BRE
ATHE

Corporeal Matters
is a publication series on arts-based research, in particular practices and concepts that place the body at the core. It illuminates how the body appears simultaneously as witness, document, and agent in contemporary life, and offers insights into corporeality as the often-neglected dimension that cuts through ethics, aesthetics, and politics. From multiple perspectives and fields of application and grounded in moments of research, encounter and debate generated in the context of the HZT-Inter-University Centre for Dance Berlin, the series hosts edited volumes, authored publications, workbooks and other formats.

Series Editors
Janez Janša, Sandra Noeth and Sandra Umathum

BREATHE
Critical Research into the Inequalities of Life

Sandra Noeth & Janez Janša (eds.)
2023

[transcript]

Content

BREATHE—An Introductory Dialogue 6
Sandra Noeth and Janez Janša

Dance and Air: About the Space between Us 16
Bojana Kunst

Abécédaire of Breathing 34
Miriam Jakob and Jana Unmüßig

Freedom of Breath 54
Francesca Raimondi

Being in the Negative 84
Basel Abbas and Ruanne Abou-Rahme

The Archive of Stolen Breaths 94
Shahram Khosravi

Meditations on Amphibiousness 112
Hope Ginsburg

Breathing Space—Germinations of Decolonial Allyship 126
Emily Beausoleil

Contributors 144

Imprint 150

Sandra Noeth and Janez Janša

BREATHE—
An Introductory
Dialogue

Janez Janša

This book opens *Corporeal Matters*, which is a publication series dedicated to research that places the body at the core. In the following dialogue, Sandra and I will follow a key principle and working modality of the series by translating oral and performative knowledge to the written word. We will introduce the idea of breathing, the topic that runs through all contributions gathered in this volume, connecting a vital, physical act to fundamental questions about life and its inequalities.

Sandra, what were the initial areas of interest that you had in mind when designing the *Breathe* lecture series at the HZT-Inter-University Centre for Dance Berlin[1] in 2018, before the idea of a book was even on the table?

Sandra Noeth

In recent years the attention that was given to breathing as a practice and as a concept across different disciplines has certainly intensified, engaging, for instance, with concerns related to environmental justice, debates on decoloniality, ongoing experiences of police and state violence and, at the same time, a renewed attention to practices of care and healing. Against this backdrop, my curatorial approach has been grounded in observations made on the body on a smaller scale, on a mundane level—small, often hardly noticeable experiences of being in or out of breath, of holding the breath—that bring questions about how our lives are conditioned in unequal ways.

One entry point is body techniques in artistic as well as therapeutic contexts such as anti-discrimination work or when dealing with stress, trauma, and anxiety. These are somatic or visceral approaches that allow

---

[1] The SODA lecture series *Breathe* at the HZT Berlin took place online in the winter term 2020/21 with invited guests Basel Abbas & Ruanne Abou-Rahme, Hope Ginsburg, Miriam Jakob & Jana Unmüßig, Maikon K., Bojana Kunst, Francesca Raimondi and Vanessa Eileen Thompson. It was curated by Sandra Noeth.

a body and a person to settle, relax, or prepare for and act in a certain situation. When practising or observing this type of breath work, I kept thinking about how its grounding and empowering potential might eventually turn into the opposite: threatening to tame a body, a voice, in a physical, but also symbolic sense, keeping them calm, under control, silent.

Furthermore, with the collective experience of the COVID-19 pandemic, breathing became key in controversial discussions about how to protect oneself and others, but also about who to protect and from whom to withdraw protection individually and collectively. Depending on the intersection of factors ranging from class, gender, wealth, migration background and others, a person's capacity to breathe clearly reveals that we are not all disposed of the same conditions to keep ourselves and others secure. At the height of the pandemic I also remember catching myself holding my breath in the underground train or when passing another person, corporeally deciding whose breath I exposed myself to and which one I avoided. Did certain bodies not seem healthy or trustworthy or safe enough? Did they represent a risk or even a threat to my body's integrity? That's a super uncomfortable and important place to navigate, as it puts you in touch with your own stereotypes and judgements and demonstrates how powerfully politics operate on the most intimate level, that of your own body. That's actually where inequality and privilege are performed and maintained.

Another impulse to dig deeper into the matter of breathing was linked to moving through urban landscapes in different geopolitical contexts, recollecting and remembering the dust—or sand or exhaust or industrial fumes—that settles in the pores of the skin and lungs, impacting a body, and reminding us of how breathing is also an indicator of environmental conditions with all their neo-capitalist and colonial inscriptions.

For me, taking on these instances and relying on the body as a perspective and as an approach to research is very valuable as it allows us to move between theoretical reflections and practical experience and to connect to something that we all know and recognize. It is also about staying with the ambivalences and asymmetries that the idea of breathing carries at the outset. The artists and theorists I invited to the lecture series took these moments as a starting point for their contributions.

Janez Janša

I agree, in breathing, in tuning in or avoiding someone's breath, there is a certain production of the other as a threat but also at times, as an ally. One important question for me arises with the act of purposefully and actively preventing somebody from breathing. This has been widely discussed in the context of police violence for instance, highlighting the physical techniques that are used to suffocate and ultimately kill those that matter less to the police. It is where the violence and discrimination that are deeply anchored in our societies are acted out on bodies. I am also thinking about the relation between language and breathing in these situations, how the repetition of the last words "I can't breathe", initiates a process in which the victim of police violence is silenced, in a literal and in a semantic sense. It is a drastic example in which the taming that you mentioned turns into silencing and where a person's breath cannot any longer be used to speak up and express themselves. What we hear and also imagine, is deeply emotional, it's a cry.

Depriving somebody of breath is depriving them of being a subject. People who assume a mandate in the institutions of repression are trained to suffocate others. They're trained to protect law and order by performing violence. This is the fundamental horror on which modern state apparatuses are built.

Sandra Noeth
The aspect of training is very significant indeed. That this is something that you systematically learn on a practical level, learning about a body's anatomy, its reactions, both to revitalize bodies, but also to very efficiently kill them. It is not about individual cases—'exceptions' or 'accidents'—but about practices that are embedded in our systems and institutions as well as in our imaginations and our bodies. For example, in public space, when hearing another person's breath or being close enough to sense and smell it, the way we relate to others, or recognise and value them, is negotiated with bodily means and does not directly translate into verbal language—which is still the language of politics, the language of law. There is also a strong element of rhythm involved in breathing, of synchronizing oneself with others, changing intensity and depth. How can breathing become the evidence of these social and cultural dynamics, not in terms of promoting the body as a vehicle of authenticity or truth, but as a way of acknowledging and learning about what might be overlooked or dismissed otherwise?

Janez Janša
The question is also how to deal with the physical reactions you mention. Do they lead us to take care of those we fail to detect and recognise? That makes me think about how listening to the different rhythm of another's breath influences and challenges our bodies as well. It's not necessarily a conscious decision but one that happens on a somatic level. Breathing

has a contagious dimension—you have no choice but to react to someone's breathing next to you.

Breathing is a vital fact, something that assails you when you are born, you are impacted with air into your lungs, you are pushed into life. Or to put it better, you are pushed into a social life, life as a social category. You transit from a pre-social life, from waters and liquids to a social life in the air. The air that cannot be private or privatized—unlike water resources that have been massively privatized. Breathing is a social tie, it is how you enter into a community and in that sense, it is a political matter.

Breathing is a social act and like other social acts, it enacts regulation and punishment by individualizing people in order to mark and identify responsibility. In a state of emergency, like a pandemic, the breath is taken out of circulation by masks for instance. You are asked to breathe the air you exhale, a mixture of the carbon dioxide that you produce and the oxygen that manages to penetrate the filter. During the COVID-19 pandemic, the contagious notion of breathing was radicalized, institutionalized. Bodies were turned into both targets and weapons. Masks were used as a shield and to disarm breath and to instigate a performance of discipline and obedience, a performance of self-protection and protection of the others, a performance of solidarity and care. This social, collective dimension of breathing is one of the key topics that runs through the contributions in this book.

Sandra Noeth
Yes, breathing is instrumental in forming collectivity. When being exposed to one another, exclusions and inclusions are implemented and marked corporeally. At times these are in tension with our individual decision-making processes and choices. Most controversial types of relations are negotiated—attraction and desire, distance, protocols and conventions. In this sense, what happened during the pandemic was about renegotiating social contracts in a performative way and I am thinking about how, in response to changing politics of proximity and distance, new choreographic patterns pretty rapidly emerged in public space. It was interesting to observe the impact of general medical politics as well as border politics on our bodies, on a micro level.

Janez Janša
I would add that when we visit the theatre, cinema, church or other large indoor gathering, we are often in situations in which we are close to the breath of people we don't know. In relation to collectivity, there are expressions in some languages that suggest "breathing as one", that is

to express the homogeneity or harmony of a group. These expressions describe the synchronization and alignment of bodies and voices in the process—as well as the risk of equalizing them. Alongside the technical aspects of taking a breath that might help to reduce stress or anxiety for example, breathing is also a social and political metaphor and not a neutral one. When suggesting that someone "take a breath" or "just breathe" before making an important decision, conditions are always set (and supervised) by the one suggesting, producing an unequal position in regard to taking or holding a breath. Again, we are not far from another facet of silencing.

To breathe is also to make a space for something and someone that is there, but also to make a space for something and someone—new or different—to emerge. In editing the book we wanted it to breathe, for the texts and their authors as well as for the readers.

Finally, breathing is not to be understood as a solely positive feature. It can also work against you, it can dysfunction and damage your body. Hyperventilation would be an example of this.

Sandra Noeth

In this sense, "taking a breath" perhaps marks a moment of criticality, a moment of interrupting narratives or affects—of interrupting ourselves. There is also an ethical dimension to this, where on a corporeal level our own convictions, values, references, roles or judgements are interrupted, and alternatives are opened up in which you interrupt yourself. But again, who actually has this possibility? The conditions of engaging with breathing this way when living conditions are so existential is such that there is no decision to make, no time to dedicate to it. This not only refers to life threatening situations such as those we mentioned before but also to everyday lives that are so packed, so full of obligations and precarious that no pause, no hesitation, no revisiting is possible. Again, this is a structural matter.

Janez Janša

I think that is actually the point. Who has the right to pronounce, "take a breath", who has the privilege to do so? When thinking about the first phase of the pandemic, for a moment it looked like the entire world was taking a breath (those who could still take one), having a break, getting away from hectic routines and so on, without really understanding that those who could take a breath accelerated the impossibility of that for those who couldn't. It is in breathing, in this vital act, that inequalities are placed. It tells us a lot about social encounters and social codes and conventions as well. Breathing is a means of communication but also a biopolitical technology.

Sandra Noeth
Yes, what finds expression here is embodied and incorporated knowledge, based on how we have learnt to read but also to imagine bodies. Aligning or disrupting bodies through breathing and movement can be both a source of resistance and empowerment, but also an act of tyranny at times. And the inscription of these politics is highly performative and highly efficient. It is linked to how bodies appear and are represented in public as well as in private space. It also trains social conventions in the aesthetic realm. Concretely, I am thinking of how dance handles breath in very different ways. These can be practices and traditions that aim at hiding breath from being audible, accentuating the formal qualities of movement, covering up exhaustion and fatigue. And then there are other approaches that work with it as a compositional element, taking on the affective and energetic dimension of breathing as a way of giving presence to the body and its lived experience. What is important here is to let go of any kind of ableist and essentialist understandings of the body and to acknowledge the ambivalence and tensions that become tangible or perceivable in breathing. To look at the different ideologies of the body as well as normative understandings of what it should look like, move like, etc. What finds expression here exceeds the artistic; it is actually about which bodies and experiences can be present in society at a certain moment in time.
Maybe this is where art can come in as well, as a critical work to do on our collective imaginaries, as a part of the system that distributes visibility and agency. It also raises questions about how we contribute to silencing or to giving attention to these voices and to the breathing?

Janez Janša
Indeed, when moving outside of the aesthetic realm, the performativity of breathing and its social and political implications make me think about much more terrible moments where breath is taken away from bodies. Ongoing tragedies where people in migration and forced displacement collectively have their breath taken away. They are deprived of air, of oxygen, suffocated, unable to breathe. This is happening now, as we speak, in trucks and other vehicles used for illegal journeys, in boats, drowning in the Mediterranean, for example. They are silenced and framed as one collective body, anonymized, existing only as numbers and statistics.

Sandra Noeth

It is very important to understand what happens here when breathing—something that is often considered an individual act, an act that gives life—is turned into a brutal act of suffocation. There are also other examples where breath is targeted directly, in which people and their territories and environment are poisoned and infected, where breathing literally becomes impossible, but also over a long period of time, often affecting generations to come. Different authors in the book take this as a springboard to explore the relation between human and non-human bodies in new ways, and to think about nature for instance, from decentralized, non human-centered perspectives.

Bodies are denied oxygen, the very possibility to live. In the process, they are often anonymized and represented as objects or masses in the generic images and narratives that we produce every day. You rarely see the individual faces of people being killed in this way or read about their individual stories. They are expunged in a legally produced state of vulnerability, taken away from the right to breathe. These highly elaborate mechanisms are instrumental in contemporary types of warfare that don't focus on the direct targeting and killing of people but on making bodies disposable, withdrawing rights, attention, care and resources from them, including the possibility to breathe.

Sandra Noeth and **Janez Janša**

Bojana Kunst

Dance and Air: About the Space between Us

> "I would like to measure my breath in relation to the air between us"
> — John Cage in a letter to Merce Cunningham, 1944

Introduction: Opening the Windows

I started writing this essay during the first wave of the pandemic, when at the institute where I teach, like many other institutions adapting to the pandemic, we were working on rules that would make it possible to have at least some practical live theatre and dance classes. We measured the distances between moving bodies and the volume of the room, between the intensity of the movement and the number of participants, we calculated the distances in relation to the breathing of the bodies regarding their dancing, talking, shouting, or being still. Only in this way, could we form small groups to safely move and work together in the space with constant ventilation and the use of medical masks. At the time I am finishing this text, such an organisation of bodies is still the main possibility for gatherings of groups of people in one space. It contributes not only to a sense of security, but also regulates and keeps the pandemic under control, only in this way can the spread of the virus be contained and broader social solidarity performed. At the heart of pandemic management is not only hygiene, but also a choreographic knowledge: the organisation of the movement of bodies, of preventing and redirecting movement, of avoiding the proximity and adjusting the distance between bodies, constantly improvising with the choreography of the "contactless" movement by keeping a permissible distance and enough air between the bodies. This knowledge is at work at the level of everyday life; when, for example, we organise our queuing in the supermarket, when we mark the chairs we can sit on in theatres and cinemas. In addition, it is at work in the political and social sphere, where pandemic organisation is often exploited for political purposes, like the temporary closure of borders, stopping the migration flows, etc. At first sight it seems that the pandemic has made the air more visible, that perhaps we are now more aware that there is no empty space between the bodies, maybe we can even bind ourselves more closely to the air, to that invisible substance without which we would not exist. However, breathing rarely becomes visible through the formation of distance; on the contrary, distance offers us all too often the sensation of a disembodied breath, an exchange of breath we can control, as if there were an empty space between us, which we can easily manipulate. For breathing is materialised through the proximity of the breath, through this intimate immersion in a fundamental reciprocity with the bodies and beings of this world. It is precisely because of the regulation of the proximity of the breath that, under the pandemic conditions, the social and economic differences between bodies are aggravated and power and hierarchies are not excluded from the pandemic regulation of distances; this regulation by no means has the same consequences for all. The pandemic has restricted the right of movement of bodies to avoid the mixture of air but this constraint is not equally distributed and it exacerbates existing social and economic differences between bodies. It has also affected the students and their study process in our institute in an uneven way. Despite all the rules we had in place to allow us to carry out at least some practical classes, it has separated and isolated some of our students from their studies, who, despite having passed the entrance exam, have been unable to obtain a student visa in countries where embassies have simply closed. At the same time, many have been forced into various precarious relationships, facing insecurity, loneliness and economic instability.

One short phrase from John Cage has often come to my mind when we were drafting these rules to make dance lessons as safe as possible. It is a short passage from the wonderful letters to his intimate and artistic partner, the choreographer Merce Cunningham. In 1944, after a long absence, Cage asks Cunningham a question about when he will be back in the September of that year, apologising for his impatience. "I would like to measure my breath in relation to the air between us".[1] I thought about how Cage expressed his desire for Cunningham's return and proximity with the measure of the breath. He had a different aim from ours, we were measuring the distances between bodies for the "safe" dance and movement. We wanted to measure the space as far as the breath reaches, so that we could put ourselves safely outside it and dance in the space beyond the reach of our breath. Cage, on the other hand, wanted to measure the breath in order to dissolve the distance, finally exchanging the volume of air between both of them in a single breath. Cage thus refers to the measure of breath as the ultimate measure of the airy reciprocity between bodies, which is not only a measure of distance or proximity, but above all a measure of quantity, of volume of air, surrounding the fitting airiness of bodies. Cage's letter is a declaration of love and the measure of breath in the letter is a reflection of the desire for the co-presence of bodies, yet this sentence can be read from a broader perspective, as an affirmation that there is no empty space between us. There is always already that element of air between us, whose quantities and volumes are countless, we are continuously

---

[1] John Cage and Mark Swed, *The Selected Letters of John Cage,* ed. Laura Kuhn, Annotated edition (Middletown, CT: Weslyan University Press, 2022), 71.

immersed in the measure of the breath around us. Such a relation to the measure of air is crucial when we speak of breath as a metaphor for social, institutional and political life. Breathing here opens up an entry into a fundamental physiological, material and corporeal reciprocity, where it is not so much a question of distance or proximity of breath (both of which can be loving, but also violent), but of a fundamental interdependence with the breath of the other, and especially of the vegetative world. We live in a profound dependence on this element of air that is both planetary and intimate, we are part of the moving volumes of air and it is this reciprocity that determines the relationships between us.

Dance and Inhalation

In the modern history of humanity, this reciprocity is not as obvious as it seems at first sight. In Western philosophy, air rarely influences how we perceive the world and ourselves in it, even though it is the most basic sensation of the body, its fundamental condition. For the space of modernity, in which modern art and science take place, and through which many institutions of art have been formed, is more empty than full. It is often an airless, static space, a space yet to be inhabited, filled and transformed, with ideas, mind, inspiration, spiritual development, reason. However, precisely these creative capacities of the human get their names from the element of air, the one that has remained largely invisible, intangible and indeterminate throughout the history of Western humanity. The ancient Greek word *pneuma* means breath, and is used in the ancient Greek context in a physiological sense, but also in a spiritual and philosophical context. In the philosophy of the Stoics, *pneuma* becomes a key cosmological principle, it is the name given to the breath of life, which arises as a mixture of air and fire, and organises both cosmic and earthly life. Breath is also in the origin of the word for soul (*psyche*), which according to some interpretations, means life, and according to others is derived from the verb to blow (*psycho*).

Even if the airiness, gust of wind, puff, breeze and breath are in the core of the human being, at the same time they often remain separate from the common windy and airy substance of the world. We are living in a world, which is generally unconcerned with breathing. We could live and relate to the world very differently if breathing would more often enter our political, social and aesthetic imagination, if it would become their main characteristics. Breathing through the history of modernity is namely too rarely a political and ethical category to manage conflicts and our social relations, and rarely serves as a metaphor when imagining the institutions and modes of working together, it is rarely a category to which we turn when organizing our educational or art institutions. Even if the act of breathing is contained in the expression of spirit, the word is often used as a metaphysical category, which divides the human being and the soul of the human from the animal and vegetal world. In this sense, breathing as a sharing act is made invisible: it is through the spirit actually that human being gets a divided (and privileged) relation to air. Michael Marder writes that breath is actually a spirit through which the air wants to be dominated; spirit is "indefinitely delaying the instant of exhalation".[2] The long breath of inhalation (inspiration), writes Marder, wants to dominate the air around us, because spirit arrives from the disembodied way of approaching the breath in the Western culture. The most destructive consequence coming out of this disembodied image is the cut in the reciprocity of the breath, the interrupting of the sharing of the breath. The result of such a disembodied approach to the breath is a neglect of the breathing surface of the body, cultivating only the inner spirit of the body, as if the breath only resided inside us. At the same time, such understanding in philosophy and science enables neglect of the respiration of plants, on which we depend as human beings. Many art institutions of modernity are organised around long breath, attending to artistic creativity and imagination as inspiration. However, inspiration, which is another word for inhalation, constitutes only part of breathing, related very often to the singularity and exceptionality of the human being. It would be much more in accordance with poetic and imaginative acts if their breathing would be organised around conspiration (breathing together), which is often at the core of the experimental and institutional changes in the 20th century, especially with communal, collaborative and open processes in the creation of art. But it is similarly necessary to think about exhalation (breathing out), which came to the centre of thinking with more recent ecological crises, climatic changes and general economic conditions of inequality, which we also have to think in the relation to the air (toxic environments, dense atmospheres, etc.). It is namely obvious how, with the climatic changes, the human expiration is not reciprocal, but literally works as *expiration* (erasure), causing damage to the airiness and well-being of the planet.

A good example of the spirit's disembodied relationship to the breath comes from the history of dance, especially in how dance achieved its institutional visibility and artistic recognition in the 17th century, at the beginnings of modernity with the establishment of academy for dance and early modern dance notations. Dance here appears as part of the cultivation of nobility and spirit of the body, which joins movement with transcendence and the metaphysical dimension of the body.

---

[2] Luce Irigaray and Michael Marder, *Through Vegetal Being: Two Philosophical Perspectives* (New York (N.Y.): Columbia University Press, 2016), 123. Here Marder refers to the sentence of Emmanuel Levinas: "spirit is the longest breath there is." See: Emmanuel Levinas, *Otherwise than Being or Beyond Essence,* trans. Alphonso Lingis (Pittsburgh, PA: Duquesne University Press, 1998), 182.

This is achieved through the strictly codified, choreographed moves and gestures of the dancing body in ballet. Even in one of the earliest notations of dance, in the notations of the choreographer and dance master Raoul-Auger Feuillet (1700), which date back to the beginning of the modern western age, the breath is not present. What is written down are the steps and hand gestures, the directions and the turns.[3] The dance steps take place along with the positions of the hands and the body, all set in a space that is in the beginning as empty as the sheet of paper was before the dance was written on it. On this sheet of paper, the dance has an end and a beginning. It is directed by the gaze of the spectator (in this case the king), which is why the sheet of paper must be turned and placed correctly in the empty space, to start the dance properly. But there is no record on this paper of the breathing of bodies, no way to grasp the flow of air, the atmosphere, the temperature, when the gasping and frazzled bodies began to warm up, and so to mix the air currents, with inhaling, exhaling and sweating, with flushed cheeks, raising dust and circulating the scent of candles. Breath is absent, invisible, like the air in between the bodies. For it seems as if the dance must slip away in a single breath, from the beginning of the movement to the gaze of the ruler, as if the spirit itself, that infinite holding of the exhalation, was actually dancing. This holding back is not only a consequence of the accomplishment and culture of the dancing body, but also a consequence of the fact that in the atmospheric environment of absolutism, through which organised bodies moved, air was often scarce, and to breathe deeply, to take in air at liberty, was not easy. We can guess that along with pleasure and artistic creation, a lot of anxiety and discomfort was present in the space, sweating and holding one's breath while maintaining a dance posture. The anxious suffocation did not just come from too much physical exertion, but from the fear of the constellation of powers and arrangements in space, the fear of the tenuous balance of powers, the tricky exchange of gaze between ruling and ruled bodies, which could also fatally fall apart at any moment during the performance. In this way, dance notation is not able to notice the insolent, stolen and rebellious breaths, because at first glance it seems as if nothing is stirring around the dancers, as if there is nothing between the bodies, the bodies are in fact dancing through one single breath.

Although the breath is crucial for the movement of bodies, its record is often absent in the institutional life of artistic dance. In its notations we barely find hints about this primary force of life that actually propels bodies into movement, is part of the movement capacity of the body, and ultimately at the core of dance techniques, of every movement inspiration. The flow of breath is so self-evident

---

[3] Raoul-Auger Feuillet, *Chorégraphie: ou, L'art de décrire la danse par caractères, figures et signes démonstratifs* (Paris: Chez l'auteur et chez Michel Brunet, 1700).

and essential to movement (and life) that it is this very self-evidence that makes it invisible. But perhaps the breath is also unworthy of dance notation, because it discloses something other than the spirit, something other than the body's elevation and separateness; it brings something intimate, hidden, but also nebulous, mismatched and swampy, something communal and dependent. In addition, the body, when it breathes, cannot quite be put into empty space and controlled, it slips out, albeit invisibly, through its own semi-corporeal and mismatched breath. This is also why we often encounter the silent body in the history of modern dance and ballet. Its silence is even more intriguing because when the body dances, it resonates, it necessarily becomes audible. We can not only hear its swishing and shuffling as it moves the air masses, but also its exhalation. The more airless and breathless it is, the more it gives way to the voice. Every voice of the dancing body happens in close entanglement with the breath. What overrides the breath of the body is precisely the spirit, through which the body slides between power relations and their disciplines, suppressing its voice and often hiding the breath under virtuosity. In this way, in the modern history of artistic dance, we often find on stage the able bodies, not those that are breathing loudly, let alone left breathless, they are voiced out, attuned to the breath of the world.

With dance techniques and disciplines of controlling the breath, the body not only dances better and can do more, it often silences the echo of what the philosopher Drew Leder calls the hinge of the breath: that twist between the outside and the inside of the body, where the body is continually fused with the world, immersed in it. Although this fusion seems intangible, characteristic of all living beings, each breath is also specific, dependent on the world and at the same time deeply intimate. Breathing is often something we are not even aware of (especially when we are not running out of it), a physiological impulse that we share as living beings, and yet it makes us singular, it is something most internal to us. Drew Leder writes, "The breath, as I will trace out, serves as a living hinge interfacing between the conscious and unconscious body, the voluntary and involuntary; physical dualities (such as left and right nostril, nose and mouth, chest and abdomen); the local and expansive act; movement and stillness, the flow of receiving and returning (inspiration, expiration); and finally, the visible and invisible (material and immaterial realms)."[4] Dance practices which remain outside institutionalised and artistically elevated choreographic notations, like ritual, folk, popular but also some experimental and expanded dance forms, take place precisely at this hinge. It seems that in these dances the body is often actually liberated through the visibility of the breath, and gets the voice with breath. Through dance this hinge becomes amplified and the body can exhale in the reciprocity with the world. In this way, dance

---

[4] Drew Leder, "Breath as the Hinge of Disease and Healing", in *Atmospheres of Breathing* (SUNY Press, 2018), 220.

actually happens in the midst of the mixing of the masses of air. For, as the philosopher Michael Marder writes, breathing can only happen in the *interstice* (which is another description for the hinge of the breath), through which the sphere of being can be amplified and enlarged.[5] In the interstice, the breath is shared and common and any separation of the breath, on the contrary, causes suffocation and lack of air. Thus the dance happens entangled with the atmosphere, it strengthens the breathing mass of the body, which with its breath is immersed in the air. Dance can thus give voice to the breath; gives it weight and intensity, entangling the breath in a loop of reciprocity between outside and inside, no longer delaying its exhalation but filling space and amplifying the world between us. Here the body is resisting the silent discipline of the breath, and reinforcing the materiality of the breath, its rhythmic flow and the production of energy, heat, atmosphere, exchange and entanglement with the environment. At the same time, it offers a voice to the breathless body. This breathless body is, despite the brevity of the breath, moving and sharing its breath with the world. In this sense, it also intervenes in the notion of virtuosity and the body's abilities, opening up worlds for movements that go beyond the silence of continuous movement. It is for this reason that the unrestrained, loud breath is often attributed to the wild, animal region of the body, becoming part of its eroticisation or exoticisation, or glimpsed as the breath of a body that cannot manage, that is incapable of going along with the illusion of ability. Because all these bodies are unwilling to be silenced, reluctant to close the gap with the world, they must be made silent by discipline, invisibility, erasure, even violence. The silencing of the breath seeks somehow to deny that every being (not only human) is unique, and wants to unify bodies through discipline and virtuosity, which on the other hand affirms the autonomy of the mind and spirit. However, as the philosopher David Abram writes, a being is never unique because some "autonomous thought is held inside its particular body or mind. Rather, each engages the common awareness from its own extraordinary angle, through its particular senses, according to the capacities of the flesh".[6] It is this common awareness of the breath that gives us our uniqueness, because we are always participating in it according to the substance of which we are made, dependent, on the vegetative world for example, which is the source of our autonomy. In this sense, the breath is the fundamental interstice of the world, because we are constantly entering into reciprocity with the environment, sharing the world through the specific flow of our life and its dependence on the air.

And this is probably why it is so difficult to dance in pandemic times. The epidemiological explanation is based on counting aerosols, those solo particles of water and air, but at the same time, the problems with dance and air have deeper causes,

---

[5] Irigaray and Marder, *Through Vegetal Being*, 124.
[6] David Abram, "The Commonwealth of Breath", in *Atmospheres of Breathing* (SUNY Press, 2018), 267.

which have seen many disciplinary expulsions of breath from dance throughout history. Dance is indeed only possible as being part of the airiness of the world, it only happens in dependence on its volume, and it is difficult to distinguish between dance and the measure of breath. In this sense, dance is a substance that modifies the atmosphere, its density and intensity; it actually participates in the movement of air masses and influences the reciprocity of breathing. The articulation of the breath is not located in a certain place in the body (the throat or the nostrils), but concerns the whole body. In dance, we are thus more akin to the breathing of plants, which at first sight seems a paradoxical statement, since plants are supposed to be static, while dance is connected with movement. However, it is precisely this difference between the human capacity for movement and the immobility of plants, which has led many philosophers to deny the possibility of plants also having a soul. The sedentary nature of plants is only apparent. It is more that their movement is invisible to human eyes and their pace and rhythm is linked to their openness to the world. As Michael Marder writes, "plants are completely exposed to the atmosphere, which they replenish with oxygen, plants breathe through their entire extension, and most of all through the leaf".[7] The body, when it dances, rather than denying its breath and pushing it inwards, dwells in the world with the whole body, and in this way, like a plant, it grows, it is open to the currents of energy, the intensity of the atmospheres and of the breath. In this sense, Cage's statement has a further dimension. The measure of the breath, and with it the air between bodies, can only be grasped with the whole body, because the body does not only breathe with the lungs, on the inside, but also with the skin, on the outside, in contact with the world to which it is always complementary.

The Exhalation of Dance

If dance does not deny breathing, it often reveals how we are always already immersed in breath, in an airiness that is always already the breath of someone else, whether human or animal, and above all of the plant world. We are always in a deeply intimate, mundane relationship with the world; we are an intimate but also negligible part of the vegetative soul of the world. Is not the measure of breath in fact our basic relationship with the world, with existence in general? After all, is it not every dance step, every movement, possible precisely because of this measure of breath, this constant exchange of the quantity of air that circulates between bodies, human and more than human? This proximity of course, has different qualities, atmospheres and intensities, it can be light or heavy, violent or loving, hot or

---

[7] Michael Marder, *The Philosopher's Plant: An Intellectual Herbarium,* Illustrated edition (New York: Columbia University Press, 2014), 216.

cold, sultry, cloudy, clear or draughty, clean or toxic, this measure, whatever it is, is always full of air, there is no empty space between us. In this sense, the choreography is more than just the organisation of movement in time and space, it must be thought of much more atmospherically, as a constant sharing of air, inhaling and exhaling, moving air masses, winds, as a gasp of wind, as a creation intimately connected to the flow of breath and reciprocity with the world. So how would the view of choreography and dance change if, rather than controlling movement, we link them to the cultivation of breath?

One of the windiest, atmospheric choreographies is at work in the short dance film by Joan Jonas, which caught my eye many years ago when I saw it in a museum, on a small screen attached to a pillar. The film, entitled *Wind*, is one of the earlier works of the experimental artist, made in 1968. As the artist states in the presentation of her work, the film is based on a performance she first made in the theatre, where she tried to combine the visual image with the living body, to create a kind of visual haiku.[8] Joan Jonas is a representative of American experimental art, and in her work, she combines different elements, media and processes, exploring their transformations, always keeping in the foreground the materiality of the medium and the environment in which her works take place.[9] It is for this reason that her early performances are often uncontrolled, and the chance encounters of materials, environments and bodies alter the perception and presence of the viewers. In her early works, she collaborated with artist-friends rather than professional dancers. It was with them that she set off for the Long Island coast in 1968, coincidentally on one of the coldest and windiest days of the year, and it is this day that gives the title to this dance film: *Wind.* In it, we find a choreographic structure in which the dancers move in groups, or in pairs. They walk across the beach, leaning back on each other and carrying the weight of their bodies, wearing mirrors hung over their clothes. All this happens in the midst of a fierce wind, a blizzard that not only constantly moves and waves their clothes, but also affects the movement of

---

[8] Bergen Kunsthall, *Platform: Joan Jonas*, 2011, https://vimeo.com/20412896.

[9] Her early works undergo various iterations and adaptations, depending on the space and medium in which they are performed. A series of her early works, entitled *Mirror Pieces,* made in the late 1960s, includes the dancers who carried and moved with large mirrors in large gyms, reception rooms and even outside. With mirrors and their reflective, fragile, breakable materiality, she wanted to alter the way movement is perceived, changing the perception of distance and the role of the audience, who could see themselves in the mirrors, as Joan Jonas writes, she wanted to turn the space into a cubist kaleidoscope. Her work *Jones Beach Space* (1970), explores distance and the audibility of sound, the way it can travel between performers and spectators, the dancers in this work producing sound with wooden squares, or circling on a six foot metal hoop through the sonic environment of the seashore. Her 1972 work *Delay Delay* undergoes several iterations in which we encounter all these elements again, through which she explores the delay of sound. She herself describes a scene from this work that was particularly dear to her, and which reveals to us how crucial the environment was. This performance took place at a festival in Rome, with the performance on one side of the Tiber River and the audience on the other. In one of the scenes, Joan Jonas together with another performer was seated in a boat that was slowly propelled by the river towards the rapids. Just when they reached them, the partner grabbed the oars and quickly rowed back to the starting point, and then the whole scene repeated again. See: Joan Jonas, "Space, Movement, Time", in *Joan Jonas* (Milan: Charta, 2007), 48–68.

their bodies. The whole work has a shaky, flickering quality, and although there is no sound in the documentation, there is no feeling of silence, the intensity of the movement of the air masses and its effect it has on the movement of bodies, is too strong. The wind influences the series of steps and movements, diagonals and assemblies of bodies, bending them, determining their pace and direction, fluttering their clothes, challenging their gravity, but also lifting the snow, churning the sea, creating waves and moving the clouds above them. Two of the dancers are equipped with mirrors, which they wear on their coats and which at times reflect this atmospheric world surrounding the performers. They move sometimes by changing their coats fluttering wildly in the wind. There is something ritualistic in this work; the film has a planetary effect because it is immersed in the world in such a simple but unique and total way. In one of her texts, Joan Jonas also speaks of her works as contemporary rituals, especially when she describes the materiality of the environment, the relationships between elements, time and space. This planetary force of the wind, which rules here, forms the fundamental movement substance of this film, while the bodies follow abstract and geometric instructions, which, due to the force of the wind, always turn into something new and unknown. This choreography is full of air, of that common medium of all-living and non-living things, the bodies are unsettled in their breathing between the currents of the wind, and the interstice of the breath of the world becomes visible in its mutuality and intensity.

David Abram writes about the role of wind in the cosmology of the Inuit and Yupik peoples, who live in the circumpolar arctic, where air is an enigma and plays a completely different role than in the Western world. In the modern age, precisely because of its invisibility, but also because of the separation of breathing from the body, we have very often turned the air into a junk yard, just as we have made the vegetative world invisible. In Inuit and Yupik cosmology, Abram writes, everything that exists comes from the wind; the invisibility of air is thus not a problem for those people's thinking and their perception of the world. This enigma of the air is the basis for respect and appreciation of the atmosphere; wind and air are something sacred, full of meaning and presence in their lives.[10] The name of this element in their language is Sila, with many variations in the local dialect such as Hila, Hla, Sla, Tla. This word describes the wind as the thought of the world, the origin of every breath. But Sila is not only the name of the elemental miracle of air, of the wonder of the winds that stir the air currents, but it also serves as the name for consciousness, this air element is the source of every breath and every consciousness, it is the wind-mind.[11] In this way, human beings, with their perception of the world, their breathing and being, are part of this wind consciousness, and air is

---

[10] Abram, "The Commonwealth of Breath", 264.
[11] Abram, 266.

the element that gives life to all. Although invisible, air is thus not immaterial, but is the common medium of all living and non-living, the element "in which we participate with the whole of our breathing bodies".[12] This conception is different from the understanding of breathing as a distinction and differentiation between living beings that accompanies Western modernity. The breathing as distinction closes rather than opens the interstice of breath, and thus disconnects the human being from the atmospheric essence of the world, from the vegetative soul of the world. This breathing as distinction underlies the origins of modern climatic, ecological, and human change, because it silences rather than amplifies the articulation and the totality of breathing bodies. In the modern industrial age, humans have turned the atmosphere into a huge garbage space, reducing biodiversity and impoverishing the vegetative world that allows us to breathe. We can say that air is sipped from the world through the endless inhalation of progress and any exhalation that must in the end take place, is full of litter. The exhalation is then not something reciprocal, but rather an expiration, an erasure, a toxic outburst of the dirt that has been produced in the course of the modern transformation of the world, an exhalation that we hold inside ourselves, that we want to get rid of. The film of Joan Jonas fascinates me not only with the planetary force of the wind, within which the dance takes place in deep dependence on air masses, but also with its dystopian touch. In the midst of the force of the wind, the people moving with difficulty are isolated, lonely, almost abandoned, not much is alive there, but at the same time everything is in movement. *Wind* is a film in which, through the force of the atmosphere, the emptiness of this airy volume is revealed, as if most of life on the planet had already disappeared from it, and only the wind stays. In this way, the film reminds me of the journey on the icy and empty side of the planet Gethen, which can be found in the science fiction book by Ursula K. Le Guin, *The Left Hand of Darkness*.[13] In this desolate vividness, framing the movement on the windy shore in a black and white muted manner, the choreography seems out of this world, belonging to the exhalation of the wind, the reflections and tremors of bodies left trapped on the frozen mirror, trembling reflections of the human past. However, we must not forget that the characters in the novel travel and hide in this icy surface because of their peace mission.

---

[12] Abram, 267.
[13] Ursula K. Le Guin, *The Left Hand of Darkness* (New York, NY: Ace Books, 1987).

Conclusion: Breath Cultivation

Philosopher Luce Irigaray writes that every birth requires us to breathe by ourselves. This does not mean that we actually know how to breathe, especially if we live in a culture that postpones breathing.[14] Such culture postpones the exhalation, disembodies the breathing person's communion with the world. We often have the feeling that we breathe in an artificial way; breathing is, as Irigaray states, "a crucial aspect of social and political life that my culture neglected".[15] It is important that we begin to "take care of the atmosphere and of the being that maintains in it".[16] Breathing is the struggle "at the level of life itself for appropriating the air essential to life",[17] and is, according to Irigaray, ontologically prior to any other power struggle, economic and social struggle, or rather, this struggle cannot be thought of without breathing. Thus, the ability to breathe is closely connected to the ability to cultivate an ethical and political life, since it can radically change our relationship to the world, being together, and not least how we organise our daily lives institutionally, politically and intimately. For this to happen, we also need to cultivate breathing, or in other words, to place ourselves at the service of the air masses of the world. The pandemic situation, in which we are still living at the time of writing this essay, shows us well how illusory it is to treat air in a pragmatic, technocratic way, especially if we do not cultivate the political and ethical principle of coexistence. We should turn away from the protection of the struggle for the protection of ourselves and for our own freedom, into a reciprocal flow of the divisibility of the air and the interdependent precariousness of the pneumatic beings of this world. This is why breathing needs to be constantly cultivated, nurtured, Irigaray often uses the word cultivation when she speaks of breathing. Michael Marder interprets her use of the word cultivation as "taking care of what grows" and places it in close dependence on the vegetative world. "Cultivation, then, is not the molding of *phusis*—that is to say of everything and everyone that or who grows—in accordance with the predetermined parameters or reason, or, worse yet, the violent uprooting of what grows by itself. Quite the opposite, it is the culturing of nature, for instance, by putting ourselves in our service, protecting, sharing and promoting the myriad of growths that comprise it."[18]

And because breathing is this extraordinary combination of something automatic (physiological), intimate, public and planetary, breathing is also a fundamental interspace of our institutional environments, however strange it may seem at first sight. In fact, in the organisation of our institutional environments, we have

---

[14] Irigaray and Marder, *Through Vegetal Being*, 20.
[15] Irigaray and Marder, 22.
[16] Irigaray and Marder, 23.
[17] Irigaray and Marder, 23.
[18] Marder, *The Philosopher's Plant*, 216.

more or less left airiness to the technicians, architects and engineers, who create ventilation systems and biodynamic architectures. The regulation of our breathing is left to the calculation of airflows and the adjustment of the optimality of air-conditioning systems, through which the gaps must open and close smoothly so that the space does not become too heavy. In a time of pandemic, we have mainly assumed this technical role, which otherwise remains hidden; we somehow all become masters in ventilation. However, airiness is rarely used as a matter and metaphor, with which it is possible to think about relationships, ways of working, the rhythms and atmospheres of temporary and more long-term communities and the creation and maintenance of institutions. How would these environments change, then, if we were to allow this very material measure of breath, a full volume that is already always with us, to reflect on the environments in which we live and work? What does it mean to process breath in institutional contexts, how is it actually possible to maintain the measure of breath in them? These questions often came to my mind when we were measuring air volumes in studios and planning distances between bodies. These questions are also pertinent because the vast majority of art institutions, art education programmes, rather than being immersed in the flow of breathing, are absorbed by endless bureaucratic and evaluative procedures, in accelerated and competitive production, often accompanied by exhaustion and lack of time. The atmosphere can be often dense, allergic, making it difficult to breathe. But how is it possible that they cause breathlessness, when these environments are supposed to be about exploring and opening up the possibilities of the airiness of dance and the body, exploring fresh breath, metaphorically speaking, and the experimental and exploratory environments actually want to give voice to the breath of the body? How can one understand this contradiction, which is at the core of many of these environments and results in breathing problems, from anxiety, fear of the future, chasing air because of accelerations, difficult atmospheres and relationships that from time to time erupt toxically? Here we can return to Luce Irigaray and her call to cultivate the breath, which is at the heart of every ethical and political struggle. "For lack of caring about it (about breathing), we pervert life, ours and that of all with whom we supposedly share it, because we are not able to respect, to love and to think of each other in their living otherness and give them back their own roots and growth."[19]

The dance full of breath resists the allegorical purity with which we have broken the connections of this world. Therefore, at the end of this essay, it might be useful to consider whether the immersion of dance and choreography in the reciprocity

---

[19] Irigaray and Marder, *Through Vegetal Being*, 97.

of airy elements, can also open the way to a more interdependent and reciprocal way of political and ethical being and thinking. This ethical being includes the breathing beings of this world equally, but also honours them in their specificity, the uniqueness of their breath. Dance always happens in dependence on air masses, and for this reason it can also open up more reciprocal relations to the atmosphere and the environment around us. Choreography becomes not the organisation of the body in space and time, but actually finds itself facing the conundrum of fullness: the intensity, force, heaviness, slowness, stasis, vortices, density or sparsity of the atmosphere, the thickness of the spaces in which our embodied breath happens. At the same time, this is about the breath of the whole body that breathes not only with the lungs but also with the skin. Such a body is like a plant directly exposed to the world, and breathing is at home on the whole surface of the body. In the micro-political field, breathing extends the importance of attention to atmospheres of community, whether temporary or more permanent, to the creation of social, artistic and political situations that are deeply connected to the continuous reciprocity, to the cultivation of environments where breath is not in short supply and is not a privilege. The right to breathe and the breathlessness is also a powerful driver of freedom, the breath and the blast, the circulation of the air masses are at its core, which is why the disciplining and domination of bodies is grounded on the silencing, the invisibility and the deprivation of breath. This happens through violence against bodies and environment, by creating atmospheres, environments, habitats in which it is not possible to breathe, the air becomes toxic for living beings. The violence takes place on a symbolic and material level. Since breathing is the hinge between the immaterial and the material, there is actually no essential difference between the poisoned atmosphere created by interpersonal relations and the poisoned air created by ecological waste. The hinge of the breath thus also shows us how political and social change happens right here, in this micro-political environment of the ability to breathe. The audible, breathing and breathless dance is turning this hinge and entangling the breath with the whole surface of the body. At the same time, it reveals that breathing is not only a personal matter, but also a planetary one. Breathing is a continuity with interruptions, breaks, an equilibrium between inhalation and exhalation, where each time, precisely through this moment of *stasis,* we swing into another circle of reciprocity.

References

Abram, David. "The Commonwealth of Breath". In *Atmospheres of Breathing*. SUNY Press, 2018.

Cage, John, and Mark Swed. *The Selected Letters of John Cage.* Edited by Laura Kuhn. Annotated edition. Middletown, CT: Weslyan University Press, 2022.

Feuillet, Raoul-Auger. *Chorégraphie: ou, L'art de décrire la danse par caractères, figures et signes démonstratifs.* Paris: Chez l'auteur et chez Michel Brunet, 1700.

Le Guin, Ursula K. *The Left Hand of Darkness.* New York, NY: Ace Books, 1987.

Irigaray, Luce, and Michael Marder. *Through Vegetal Being: Two Philosophical Perspectives.* New York (N.Y.): Columbia University Press, 2016.

Jonas, Joan. "Space, Movement, Time". In *Joan Jonas*. Milan: Charta, 2007.

Kunsthall, Bergen. *Platform: Joan Jonas,* 2011. https://vimeo.com/20412896.

Leder, Drew. "Breath as the Hinge of Disease and Healing". In *Atmospheres of Breathing*. SUNY Press, 2018.

Levinas, Emmanuel. *Otherwise than Being or Beyond Essence.* Translated by Alphonso Lingis. Pittsburgh, PA: Duquesne University Press, 1998.

Marder, Michael. *The Philosopher's Plant: An Intellectual Herbarium.* Illustrated edition. New York: Columbia University Press, 2014.

Miriam Jakob and Jana Unmüßig

Abécédaire of Breathing

In our collaborative project *Breathing With*[1], we engaged in our research topic of breathing in very different, yet to us equally important ways: from private exchanges on different experiences with breath, we discussed 'bigger' questions around the politics and ecologies of breathing, including theories and concepts of breath. At the same time, both of us engaged in different breathing practices in order to not lose the actual experience of creating an awareness of breath.

When Sandra Noeth invited us to participate in the lecture series *Breathe* we decided to use the form of an *abécédaire* or alphabet primer as a form that allowed us to systemise the different references, concepts and thoughts that we identified as relevant to our artistic research in that moment of our research trajectory. The strict alphabetical order gave us permission to embrace the abundance, multi-directionality and almost monstrosity of references and interests concerning breathing. We felt released by the linear form of the *abécédaire* and trusted its structure to be solid enough to carry a variety of concerns with breathing. The plurality of voices, ideas and associations was vital to the project to also let a certain tension and friction among the material take place. Tension and friction as a means to instigate listening.

Each letter entailed for us the possibility of beginning the writing again and again. The idea of a 'series of beginnings' has been a research-dramaturgy since the start of the project, yet it expresses our understanding that there are differently structured ways of knowing.

We co-wrote, combining our voices. In writing it was important to us to mark our distinct voices instead of using an idea of a 'we'. Therefore, we experimented with a 'you' or an 'I' whenever we want to emphasize the two-tone aspect of our thinking. However, the question of how we use the personal pronoun was not only a question of how we mark who is speaking but also how we disguise who is speaking. In the end, the shared writing process was also an emotional need in that period of our research. We needed to get closer and not take up the individualized artist position.

The *Abécédaire of Breathing* can be used as a score. We invite the reader to play with the chronological structure of the *abécédaire* and to start from any place in the document, to jump between the letters, go back and forth and to eventually draw lines and connections between them. The reader can also add their own thoughts and interests in the respective section of a letter. The letter B is purposefully left blank to give space to the reader to fill with their own imaginaries and urgencies.

A as in Air » Air that is never empty but alive and animated, a meeting point of different species, a habitat in its own terms.

B as in Breathing

Miriam Jakob and **Jana Unmüßig**

C as in Carrying » One important principle of perceptible breathwork is the simultaneous experience of "carrying" and "being carried",[2] a mode of perceiving circumvents dialectics in an either-or way by embracing two opposing directions and forces. This creates a certain tension that allows one both to be present and to create a constant movement between them. When I remind myself that I am carried by the stool I'm sitting on, the massage table I'm lying on, the feet I'm standing on—it produces a sensation of two surfaces meeting each other: the stool meeting my sit bones. At the same time there is a sensation almost like two magnets repelling each other as our collaborator Lisa Densem often describes it in our conversations.[3] Becoming aware of this quality is an act of remembrance: that there are always more sensations and perceptions available to us than we are usually aware of. There is a sense of weight and lightness at the same time. Carrying also reminds me of the *Carrier Bag Theory of Fiction* by Ursula Le Guin.[4] Le Guin prompts us that it is not the hero's spectacular narratives that were needed in order to survive and to co-live in a meaningful way: In the beginning it was not the spear but the carrier bag, that enabled humans to collect and to share, be it food, medicinal herbs, and also stories. Progressive utopias must inevitably lead to the abyss of violence. They leave out the experiences of quotidian, simple things. We understand breath work as a practice that enables us to create an awareness for these simple yet not easily perceivable changes in our bodies that comes with experiencing the breath as a movement, each moment anew.

Instruction by Lisa Densem (breathing practice):

"Sit on a chair or a stool with your lower legs falling down from the knee. Let both soles of your feet rest equally on the floor and your arms fall from the shoulders, resting the palms of your hands on your thighs, or cupping one hand gently in the other. Let the weight of your torso rest on your sit bones. Feel the whole weight of your body falling down through your sit bones and your feet and feel the floor and the stool rising up to support you. Feel your weight, and at the same time a sense of lightness. Allow your spine to float vertically upwards, and your skull to balance delicately and with complexity on the top of the spine. Feel the embrace of the air all around you and notice this same air coming and going as you breathe. Notice a slight pressure into the stool through your sit bones as you breathe in, and a slight loss of pressure as you breathe out. Let your breath come and go on its own and let it be as shallow or as deep as it needs to be in each moment. The movement of the breath moves your body, almost imperceptibly. Feel the whole expanse of floor and earth beneath you and sense the floor carrying your weight and your movement. Sense the floor carrying your movement through time."[5]

D as in Diluting » Diluting, the process of thinning down, or watering down a substance, is a notion that came to us when getting our heads for a short period of time into the thinking of post-colonial writer Édouard Glissant. The notion came to us through Glissant's sentence "I can change through exchanging with others, without losing or diluting my sense of self."[6] In the *Archipelago Conversations*,[7] archipelagoes are clusters of islands that are conceived as counterparts to continents. Different archipelagoes meet. Asian archipelagoes meet the archipelagoes of the Antilles. Glissant develops on that basis the utopian ideal of creolisation—where different cultures mix and create something totally new.

Let's lean back into the direction of breathing from here. What can such thought—as roughly as it is described here—allow you/me to speculate about breathing?

Mixing—in the context of creolisation—does not imply a thinning out or a diluting of one's sense of self. We pick up on this, being aware that we carry Glissant's thoughts into a different context, yet his thinking seems contemporary. It seems like it is speaking to the you/me who is looking into/*nearby* breathing. The contemporaneity of Glissant's sentence appears when thinking in post-humanist terms. Breathing as an intra-active phenomenon is a type of breathing that is entangled with the breathings of human and more-than-human agencies. My breath is changing when intra-acting with other breathings. In post-humanist terms it is less about 'exchange' since intra-action is rather close to enmeshment and entanglement. Yet Glissant's "I can change through exchanging with others, without losing or diluting my sense of self", spoke to us as another way to address how breathing doesn't happen only 'in me', but working *nearby* breathing can produce change by getting very close to others (human and non-human) "without losing (...) my sense of self."

E as in Earth » Earth is another element relevant to *Breathing With,* next to air. Air is needed to breathe but earth is too. The ground we stand on, the air that passes through our lungs and the water that we drink shape us constantly. All breathing organisms need ground, some land to breathe from. Breathing turns into a movement that happens above the ground. But what if one could breathe ground, earth, soil instead of air? Which body emerges then? What phantasmagorical anatomies arise?

According to evolutionary theorist and biologist Lynn Margulis, evolution does not correspond to the figure of a tree (as Darwin sketched) but a web.[8] Life from its very beginning was interconnected in a symbiotic act that at times generated fusions and forms we would not have imagined in the first place.

Thinking of earth as a symbiosis between living organisms is a critique of so-called anthropocentrism and individualism. The very reproducibility of our body depends on food that is edible, on air that is breathable and soil that is not completely toxic. 'We' as human animals, taking into account all the differences and inequalities that exist, need to understand ourselves as radically relational and radically interdependent. This interdependence can only exist in equality. The notion of 'equality' could be immediately challenged of course. What kind of equality? For whom, where and when?

Yet, I/you remain thinking about the visual artist Hito Steyerl saying in an interview, "People always think they feel solidarity with those who are the same, but that is a dead end. People are very different, and if they want to be in solidarity, they have to actively ignore this difference—knowing that it is then a fiction, a necessary fiction."[9]

F as in Filming » In 2020 I started to take Middendorf-sessions in perceptible breath work. I asked my artistic collaborator Felix Classen to accompany me in one session with the camera. I did not really intend to share or project the material. When I was watching the recordings, I was fascinated by how haptic the images were and the way they resonated with my questions, which were circulating around the question of transposing the bodywork that I experience into the medium of film. How can an experience and process of invisible exchange of energies be filmed? What of the 'things' that happen can be 'captured' on video? Is it helpful to zoom into closeup shots of a body moved by breath? How far does a film frame, and the steadiness of the image support seeing the movement of the air through the body?

I didn't want the film to be a documentation of a breathwork session, rather I understood the filming as an invitation to a different way of thinking. If breathing is the narrative of this video it occurs in the relationship between bodies, between the medium and the senses and between the different forms of touch and being touched. Video available at https://vimeo.com/782682971, password: Breathing_With

G as in Górska » When Miriam wrote to me around two years ago, asking for a reference on the topic of breathing, I suggested she read Magdalena Górska's publication Breathing Matters.[10] Later, when Miriam and I started our dialogue on breathing in the frame of the artistic research grant programme, the gender studies scholar Magdalena Górska was one of the main theoretical inputs that interested both of us equally.

What makes Górska interesting to you/me is that she is a contemporary voice addressing breathing within a post-humanist framework. With Górska, there is a breathing post-human subject that is always already entangled with more-than-human actants. And at the same time, she looks into specific case studies such as a sex workers' relationship to breathing. She combines a post-humanist agenda with an almost sociological interest to carve out the notion of breathing as an intra-active phenomenon. Górska's publication also includes a personal account of her panic attacks and anxieties without dismissing them as a psychological problem that needs to be solved.

gether, we found out that there is the contact between the client and the practitioner that tells the practitioner what to do, where to place the hand. Placing the hands 'intuitively' is then a relational practice of becoming-with with the client.

H as in Hands » Marion Rosen trained as a physiotherapist and developed the Rosen Method in her 50s.[11] The Rosen Method is a hands-on bodywork at the threshold of psychotherapy. She once said that it is up to her hands to decide where she would start the work or treatment. She would place her hands as if the hands had a knowledge of their own. I/you keep coming back to the knowledge of the hands because in our artistic research I/you want to approach different modalities of knowing, of creating *knowledges,* of knowledge that can be initiated by and transmitted through the hands for example.

I/you have often talked about the notion of intuition that we have a difficult time with, since it seems to perpetuate an idea of an artist genius who once was kissed by the muse and 'just follows their intuition'. You/I struggle with this conception because it is a very narrow idea of artistic practice and artistic identity. If the hands know 'intuitively' where to go, where to place them, where to stay, where to push, it is because they are always in relation to myriads of *other* senses and in contact with the person on the bench and all the other materialities at stake in the situation.

In one of the conversations between you/me and a practitioner we interviewed to-

I as in Intimacy » Intimacy and breathing produce images of closeness, or close-ups, of "haptic visuality".[12] Intimacy and breathing make you/me also think of what philosopher Francesca Raimondi described in her lecture "Freedom to Breathe"[13] as "the sound of breath", the sound before the voice takes over, before the voice colours the breath in. There is a rawness to breath's quality when described in terms of intimacy. And there is the wish of immediacy circulating when breath and intimacy are thought together.

I/you have noticed a search for that immediacy towards the ones attending some of the lectures within the lecture series *Breathe* when e.g. philosopher Bojana Kunst in her lecture "Some questions on the 'international' art education: on studying, breathing and reciprocity"[14] mentioned at the margin of her lecture about being an anxious person and Francesca Raimondi talked among many other things about her nervous system. When speaking *nearby* one's breathing it is also an offer to share an intimate knowledge which is implicit in a way one might not be aware of at all times. Sharing entails vulnerability and becoming aware of one's breathing when speaking.

Speaking about breathing brings with it a new grammar of intimacy.

J as in Joy » Often, when coming out of a Middendorf- or Rosen-breathwork session, I/you feel light and positive. The worries I/you have when entering the session have not disappeared, but I/you feel able to handle them. There is a sense of empowerment. And with lightness, there comes a gentle joy of living.

Thinking about joy and empowerment I/you think of Audre Lorde's *The Uses of the Erotic*.[15] "The erotic functions for me in several ways, and the first is in providing the power which comes from sharing deeply any pursuit with another person".[16] In somatic breath bodywork, there is such deep sharing as Lorde describes it in the quote above which makes the encounter between practitioner and client an empowering experience. Not only for the client, but also for the practitioner.

"For the erotic is not a question only of what we do; it is a question of how acutely and fully we can feel in the doing. Once we know the extent to which we are capable of feeling that sense of satisfaction and completion, we can then observe which of our various life endeavours brings us closest to that fullness."[17]

I/you believe that breathing and emotions such as joy challenge normative ways of conceiving knowledge as merely cognitive endeavours. I/you feel supported in this view when reading Lorde's writings about the "deep and irreplaceable knowledge of my capacity for joy".[18] Her way of thinking about joy makes space for an epistemology of emotions.

K as in Knowing » Breathing with awareness lets knowledge emerge. When looking at the letter J, it might be what we call an epistemology of emotions, or "tacit knowledge",[19] or embodied knowledge. Breathing as a research subject can also give insight, hence knowledge, about different livelihoods such as mine workers' or sex workers' relationship to breathing (cf. Górska).

And yet, I feel a slight discomfort with claiming how breathing creates knowledge. I am a bit tired of the constant need to produce knowledge, of the knowledgeilisation of all practices (foremost in the discussion how art creates knowledge). To write that breathing creates knowledge gives me a taste of the imperative of knowledge production in knowledge society.

At the same time, I/you would like breathing to partake in larger discursive environments and for that, it seems important to speculate that breathing can create knowledge.

Breathing-knowing hints at a porous type of knowledge, a kind of knowledge that is generated only through the embodiment of interconnection. In breathing, one is enmeshed with other breathings (human and more-than-human) which calls on a relational type of knowledge.

L as in Landscape » Lately in our research I/you used the term landscape as a figure of thought. A landscape of different knowledge that spreads out around you/me and that would allow various beginnings, many different pathways. I/you fabulate this landscape as a landscape where currents, islands and different sediments are entangled.

But where do I/you depart from within that landscape? How can I/you find a means of orientation if there is no beginning and no end?

In correspondence with breathing as a movement that ebbs and flows through the body, that entails at times resting, pauses, after which the volume of activity is taken up again. We used the gesture of meandering as a research method. Meandering is walking without a pre-made map. Instead, we create the map while mapping out the paths, while formulating/fabulating provisional conclusions.

Meandering as research creates a temporality where a constant becoming-with the act of walking creates an oscillation of partially perceived frames. This results in a kind of fractional knowledge that we accept, with its uneven rhythm, where knowing is at times a fleeting gesture. It equally calls for what social anthropologist Tim Ingold developed through the notion of taskscape: "Just as the landscape is an array of related features, so—by analogy—the taskspace is an array of related activities."[20]

Through meandering, the landscape emerges and the landscape acts back on us.

Many people are walking with us or have been walking; are creating paths simultaneously, have created paths before us.

M as in Middendorf » Ise Middendorf (1910–2009) was born in Saxony, trained in gymnastics and later continued her education with Clara Schlaffhorst and Hedwig Andersen who developed their own method of breathing and voice. Middendorf was also interested in the work of Carl Jung. Around 1935 she opened her own office in Berlin-Lichterfelde. Some 30 years later, in the 1960s, she opened the Middendorf Institute in Berlin, and in 1971 she was appointed professor at the UdK Berlin, teaching breathing and voice for actors and singers. Throughout her life, Middendorf developed the particular breath work she called *Perceptual Breathing*, which is practised in one-to-one or group situations. The guiding principle of *Perceptual Breathing* can be summarized in this way, I let the breathing come, I let the breathing go and wait until it comes back by itself.

N as in nearby » We have been researching nearby-breathing. And with *nearby,* we refer to the filmmaker, writer and decolonial thinker Trinh T. Minh-ha who said "I do not intend to speak about; just speak nearby" in her film *Reassemblage*[21].

Trinh T. Minh-ha was an important reference during my studies in anthropology. For my master's thesis I interviewed 3 friends and acquaintances about their fears and panic attacks. Later I played back to them my edited version of the interviews and filmed them listening to these edited interviews. They became their own listeners. What interested me was to create a distance to the words they had said in the interviews and play with the visual representation of their faces and bodies. My university supervisor back then found fault that my approach wasn't scientific enough. To focus on three individuals would not shed light on societal structures of fear and would therefore be insufficient for drawing any representational conclusions.

I guess the critique was that this filmic essay was poetic rather than academic. I insist on speaking *nearby* as it allows approaching a subject—whether in the context of scholarship or art. It can offer meaning in such a way that exceeds what is said or shown. "To say therefore that one prefers not to speak about but rather to speak *nearby,* is a great challenge. Because actually, this is not just a technique or a statement to be made verbally. It is an attitude in life, a way of positioning oneself in relation to the world."[22]

To use in your/my research Trinh T. Minh-ha's *nearby* felt like a necessary consequence, as breath can never be fixed. It only exists in a movement of ebbs and flows and respites. Each breath is only a moment of transition opening up to other possible moments of transition. It is like following a movement whose succession is formed by the rhythm of time passing. Following this movement *nearby* allows proximity to the person breathing. It also offers a space of "positioning oneself in relation to the world"[23] for you/me as initiators of this project.

O as in Oxygen » "In the evolutionary history of life on earth oxygen was first a toxin. Oxygen is now the most widespread element in the lithosphere and the sea, as well as the atmosphere and biosphere, but this was not always the case. Around 2.3 billion years ago, the so-called Great Oxidation Event took place, with catastrophic consequences that mark it still as the biggest extinction in earth's history. If carbon in the atmosphere now threatens life as we know it, oxygen once did the same. Some anaerobic life forms survived the catastrophic toxin, freestanding oxygen, eventually became the basis for respiration as organisms adapted evolutionarily to the new habitat, eventually becoming the dominant organisms on earth. Some anaerobic life forms survived the catastrophe and live on (i.e. Intestines) but they are no longer the dominant species on earth."[24]

In this quote John Durham Peters reminds you/me of how the history of breath started a very long time ago. It also invites you/me to acknowledge how oxygen has not always been a life-giving but was initially a life-taking element. Peters calls on your/my capacity to shift perspective and to reshuffle a seemingly taking for granted position.

P as in Painting » I started painting during my undergraduate studies in dance. Painting was a way of handling the heavy load of physical training, a means to digest all that which was triggered by physically moving and dancing. Later, I had a period studying art pedagogy in order to become a schoolteacher in visual arts, and I enjoyed painting best during that time. I still paint when I have time and energy. I consider painting one among many practices I do.

The painting practice I am interested in is limited to the canvas. I am curious how the brush meets the canvas and how the (acrylic) colour unfolds and spreads across it. I am affected by that encounter of canvas-brush-colour. From the moment *the-brush-touches-the canvas-and-the-colour-spreads,* I think of breathing.

In breathing-painting, the visible is emerging. The hand animated by the breathing of my body holds the brush and moves it, again and again, placing pigment on a surface. I think of the painter and psychoanalyst Bracha Ettinger when she writes that "You can stop painting in the middle—the thing of the painting breathes."[25]

I struggle with this vitalist projection onto painting. According to the art historian Isabelle Graw, it is due to the painting's physicality. The physicality of painting is also what makes Graw think that painting "simultaneously evokes the ghostlike presence of their absent author".[26] The author and its absence, the absence of their breath—these are bits of thoughts that come to me when engaging in thinking about breath with Graw's considerations on painting as a backdrop.

When I was choreographing actively between 2008 and 2015, I had no real need to perform physically on stage (I did perform once on stage, but I understood after that this choice came from expectations I thought others had towards me). During all these years I worked on Middendorf breathwork and I also worked with a Walter Benjamin quote. In it, Benjamin recounts a Chinese saying, in which a painter disappears into the door of a house he had painted.[27] As a choreographer, I considered being this painter, *tracing* my *disappearance* through the works. Now, many years later, I have a sense of how painting, my approach to choreography, and breathing are interrelated through the idea of time and lived time being stored in breathing, painting and choreographing as I practised it.

Q as in questions » We keep having many questions *nearby* breathing instead of one (research) question. The multitude of questions invites a speculation on a non-systematic way of doing research and makes us lean towards doing research differently. We have kept working with at times contradicting questions, open questions, complicated questions, simple questions, unanswerable questions, pragmatic questions and so forth.

Carrying and being carried by a multitude of questions, turns our endeavour into an affective rather than effective project and with that, the notion of meandering appeared in our conversations.

Excerpt of questions we asked each other. How are you? How was the breathwork session? Have you read that XY article? Could you scan the text and send it to me? When shall we meet tomorrow? Can you send a zoom invitation? Why do I feel so out of breath in a project dealing with breathing? How is that for you?

in the body. Finally, there is the verbal plane, in which while touching and observing, the practitioner also engages the client in a particular kind of conversation. In contrast to massage, in which practitioner and client sometimes also start talking during a treatment, the Rosen practitioner poses subtle questions about the mental and physical landscape of the client, while always keeping track of how words affect the body, *how speaking affects the corporeal.*

R as in Rosen, Marion » Marion Rosen (1914–2012) was a German-born, Berkeley-based physiotherapist and bodywork practitioner. She was a contemporary of Ilse Middendorf, but in contrast to Middendorf, she had to flee Nazi-Germany and migrate to the US. At the age of 50, after many years of physiotherapy practice, she finally developed her own method, the Rosen Method. When still living in Germany, she was very influenced by Lucy Heyer (1891–1991), a physiotherapist who worked with a particular focus on breathing and who often treated the psychotherapy clients of her husband, Gustav Richard Heyer. Marion Rosen was a young woman when she worked with Lucy Heyer but the combination of breathing and psychic transformation is something she included many years later in the Rosen Method. In the Rosen-method the practitioner works on a dense set of tasks: one is the observation of the breath and how breathing changes depending on touch or speech. The other one is the touch of the practitioner that searches for tension and its release

S as in Sensing » Breathing calls on creating breath awareness, which asks for sensing differently to everyday life situations. The senses, and therefore perception are, for philosopher and media theorist Dieter Mersch, not "perception-of-something"[28] or senses-of-something, but foremost perception-*that*-I-sense-something (Mersch 2002).[29] He challenges the idea of intentionality of the senses/perception because perceiving/sensing, for Mersch, brings with it the inescapability of affect, of being affected.

How can one communicate how one senses self and body after a body work session of the Rosen Method or Perceptual Breathing of Ilse Middendorf for example?

Throughout the project, we were puzzled by the concern and wish to bridge a seeming gap between personal and subjective experience in the somatic bodywork and the realm of the artistic. This is why our artistic practices are, despite all the twists and expansions, still rooted in a trained background of dance and choreography.

T as in Trust » What does trust mean in our collaboration? What does it mean to you? What does it mean to me? How does each of us experience trust? How precarious is trust? How is trust a means of thinking forward, backwards, sidewards? How is trust a way to feel?

U as in unconditioning » Breathing is conditioned by the distinct physiologies and contexts of the human and more-than-human histories. It is a phenomenon and practice encapsulated by a thick net of various conditions. The idea of 'unconditioning' is utopian, yet we keep believing that utopias in the forms of imaginaries are necessary. They are necessary to create space where conditions can—if not change entirely—be rediscovered, redone, rediscussed. That process of revisiting is the process of unconditioning we refer to here.

T as in Theory » I/You like to think of theory as an acquaintance one likes to visit once in a while. Someone/something you like to hang out with, and you like to think with. Theory as someone that unsettles one's position. But theory can also be a kind of a rebel in that sense. It reminds you that something more is always out there and is worth pursuing.

V as in Voice » "'A voice means this: there is a living person, throat, chest, feelings, who sends into the air this voice, different from all other voices (...) A voice involves the throat, saliva.' When the human voice vibrates, there is someone in flesh and bone who emits it."[30]
Although Adriana Cavarero emphasizes the uniqueness and physical materiality of each voice, she does not refer to the voice as

an essence or a secret nucleus of the self, "rather it is a deep vitality of the unique being who takes pleasure in revealing herself through the emission of the voice",[31] an acoustically perceptible breath.

During the research on *Breathing With*, I started taking singing lessons. I learned about the importance of breathing, to be in dialogue with the breath, to let air swirl through the head before a sound is emitted. Together with the singing teacher Johanna Peine, I did all kinds of different exercises in which the imaginative as a practical act was integral, in order to come closer to this uniqueness of one's voice. When opening to the voice from the practice of breathing, voice is a form of exhalation. Voicing is like 'colouring in the exhale', giving the exhalation a different grain, a different colourfulness. But at the bottom line, using the voice can still be understood as a moment of exhaling. The voice activated through thought appears in its physicality.

W as in Water » Next to air and earth, water is another element I/you consider when thinking *nearby* breathing. I/you want to understand water not as a metaphor for the "sameness project"[32] rather as an 'allowing difference'. As Astrida Neimanis suggests, water flows through and across difference: "As watery, we experience ourselves less as isolated entities, and more as oceanic eddies [...] The space between ourselves and our others is at once as distant as the primeval sea, yet also closer than our own skin—the traces of those same oceanic beginnings still cycle through us, pausing as this bodily thing we call 'mine'."[33]

W as in Writing » Writing a word carries with it an exhalation. Writing a word anticipates the exhale. I write a word for it to be read (by myself or others). Sometimes I read the word out loud, taste the word as I write it and hope that someone else might read it too. Writing contains exhaling. Writing and breathing are linked through rhythm. Rhythm precedes meaning.[34] When rhythm comes before meaning, grammar and structure need to be rethought, redone.

Writing is not a solitary practice but a practice of balancing out various entanglements, having conversation with many other humans and more-than-humans. Breathing-writing reinforces this entanglement with other materialities (human and more-than-human) because through breath I/you sense the palms of my/your hands on the keyboard of the computer in a more effective manner: Warm palms, cold palms, sweaty hands moved by the inhale and the exhale. Breathing extends from the diaphragm into the torso, into the arms, into the hands.

X as in » We could not find a notion, practitioner or author starting with the letter x that we had found relevant to *Breathing With*. We tried in writing xeno and xenofeminism, but did not make it to flesh out thoughts around these in relation to breathing.

The acknowledgement of limits and limitations are part of researching, working, pondering *nearby* breathing.

Y as in Yodeling » My yodel teacher Doreen always says that "Yodelling is so much in the moment". This is the hardest point in the process of learning how to yodel because we are all used to preparations. If you start thinking about what's next, you start preparing your vocal cords and then the sensation of yodelling doesn't happen—which is the voice break. The yodelling produces a shortcut of the voice, a sudden change in the registers between head and chest voice. This shortcut does to the voice what you usually want to avoid when speaking and singing, as the voice breaks mostly in uncontrolled situations like fear, crying or so-called hysteria.

Yo—la—la—u—di—ri
di—ri—yo—u—di
di—ri—yo—u—di—ye—i—di—yo—u—di—ye—i—di

Miriam Jakob and **Jana Unmüßig**

Z as in zooming » We mainly met on Zoom during the two years of the fellowship. We had planned to meet more often in person. I thought I would come every two months to Berlin. Maybe we would have met in the studio, maybe we would have started dancing together. But there was the pandemic and so our project was embracing and developing—more than we had planned—online formats.

Zoom became our shared studio. The notion of meandering emerged partially because we started to develop a practice online during which participants were also asked to take distance from the two-dimensional screen.

[1] The project was developed with the generous support and funding of the Berlin Artistic Research Grant Programme Berlin/gkfd 2020/2021. https://kuenstlerischeforschung.berlin (last accessed 22.9.2022).

[2] We use "carrying" in reference to Bracha Ettinger https://www.youtube.com/watch?v=A3hbix-TIncU (last accessed 21.9.2022). In addition, we reference "carrying" in relation to the vocabulary used in the *Perceptible Breath* by Ilse Middendorf (also see: Ilse Middendorf: *The Perceptible Breath. A Breathing Science*, Junfermann-Verlag, 1990). We have practiced perceptible breathwork through our collaborator Lisa Densem who is a licenced Breath Experience practitioner.

[3] Lisa Densem is a Berlin based dancer, choreographer and breath practitioner. Conversations were held with her during our artistic research project 2020/2021.

[4] Ursula K. Le Guin, "The Carrier Bag Theory of Fiction" (Terra Incognita, 2019): 25-37.

[5] Lisa Densem has written this short example of a breath instruction for this text. The text is based on what Lisa said at the performance evening *Currents of Breath*, that was performed at Radialsystem Berlin 25.-27.2.2022 in collaboration with Miriam Jakob and Jana Unmüßig, together with Felix Classen, Su-Mi Jang and Signe Lidén.

[6] "Earth is Trembling: Édouard Glissant in Conversation with Hans Ulrich Obrist", https://032c.com/magazine/edouard-glissant-and-hans-ulrich-obrist (last accessed 7.9.2022).

[7] Édouard Glissant and Hans Ulrich Obrist, *The Archipelago Conversations*, vol. 6 (New York, NY: Isolarii, 2021).

[8] Lynn Margulis, *Symbiotic Planet: A New Look at Evolution* (Basic Books, 1999).

[9] Carolin Wiedemann, "Hito Steyerl im Interview: Ist das Museum ein Schlachtfeld?", *FAZ.NET*, 27 December 2016, https://www.faz.net/aktuell/feuilleton/kunst-und-architektur/interview-mit-der-kuenstlerin-hito-steyerl-14587945.html. Translation by the authors.

[10] Magdalena Górska, *Breathing Matters. Feminist Inter-Sectional Politics of Vulnerability,* vol. 683, Linköping Studies in Arts and Science (Linköping University, 2016).

[11] Don Johnson, *Bone, breath & gesture: practices of embodiment* (North Atlantic Books 1995).

[12] Laura U. Marks, *The Skin of the Film: Intercultural Cinema, Embodiment and the Senses* (Duke University Press 2000).

[13] Francesca Raimondi, "Freedom to Breathe" (HZT Berlin, SODA-lecture series "Breathe", 25 November 2020, online).

[14] Bojana Kunst, "Some Questions on the 'International' in Art Education: On Studying, Breathing and Reciprocity" (HZT Berlin, SODA lecture series "Breathe", 18 November 2020, online).

[15] Audre Lorde, "Uses of the Erotic: The Erotic As Power", in: Ibid.: *Sister Outsider: Essays and Speeches* (Crossing Press, 1981).

[16] Lorde, 89.

[17] Lorde, 88.

[18] Lorde, 89.

[19] Michael Polanyi, *The Tacit Dimension* (University of Chicago Press 2009).

[20] Tim Ingold, *The Perception of the Environment: Essays on Livelihood, Dwelling and Skill* (Routledge, 2002): 195.

[21] Trinh T. Minh-ha, *Reassemblage: From the Firelight to the Screen*, Documentary, Short, 2016.

[22] Nancy N. Chen, "'Speaking Nearby:' A Conversation with Trinh T. Minh-ha", *Visual Anthropology Review* 8, no. 1 (1 March 1992): 87.

[23] Chen: 87.

[24] John Durham Peters, "The Media of Breathing", in *Atmospheres of Breathing* (SUNY Press, 2018): 182-83.

[25] Bracha Ettinger et al., *Bracha L. Ettinger: And My Heart Wound Space* (Wild Pansy Press 2015): 353.

[26] Isabelle Graw, "The Value of Liveliness Painting as an Index of Agency in the New Eceonomy", in: Isabelle Graw and Ewa Lajer-Burcharth, eds., *Painting Beyond Itself: The Medium in the Post-Medium Condition* (Sternberg Press, 2016): 79-101.

[27] Walter Benjamin, *The Work of Art in the Age of Mechanical Reproduction,* trans. A. J. Underwood (Penguin Books 2008).

[28] Dieter Mersch, *Ereignis und Aura*. (Suhrkamp Verlag 2002): 32, translation by the authors.

[29] Mersch: 32.

[30] Adriana Cavarero, *For More than One Voice: Toward a Philosophy of Vocal Expression,* trans. Paul A. Kottman, 1st edition (Stanford University Press, 2005): 4.

[31] Cavarero, 4.

[32] Natascha Sadr Haghighian: Parallax, 132: http://possest.de/wp-content/uploads/2016/02/Parallax_natascha_sadr_haghighian.pdf

[33] Astrida Neimanis, "Hydrofeminism: Or, on Becoming a Body of Water", in *Undutiful Daughters: New Directions in Feminist Thought and Practice* (Palgrave Macmillan, 2012), 1.

[34] Henri Meschonnic, *Critique du rythme anthropologie historique du langage* (Verdier 2009).

Miriam Jakob and **Jana Unmüßig**

Francesca Raimondi

Freedom of Breath

Back in 2016, anthropologist Elizabeth A. Povinelli observed "a potential shift in our political discourses [...] from the demand 'listen to me' to the statement 'I can't breathe'".[1] Povinelli discusses this shift as a possible effect of the anthropogenic climate change, but also of the structural racisms and (neo-)colonialism characterizing what she calls "late liberalism" to underlie the continuity of our current regime with a long history of domination of human and more-than-human beings. What in 2016 was still partly a "potential" shift—from the identity politics call for recognition to a cry against the impossibility to breathe—has become a full reality in our present: the ongoing acts of racist violence like the one on George Floyd or the mass drowning of refugees in the Mediterranean have been joined by the Covid-19 pandemic as a new variant of "Severe Acute Respiratory Syndrome", the suffocation from forest fires stretching for miles and increasing intoxication through fumes. Although the effects of these last phenomena unmistakably hit groups marginalized by age, health, class, race and gender harder, the impossibility of breathing is increasingly becoming a condition shared globally.

Late liberalism thus appears to be the regime where the economic, political and social arrangements of the capitalist, globalized world can no longer hide their violent impacts on the most visceral dimensions of the body, such as breathing. Facing the increasing impossibility to breathe, Povinelli raises a question that is more topical than ever, "Where is the human body if it is viewed from the lung?"[2] This question calls for a shift from an anthropological view that centres human existence in speaking and working capacities, to one that focuses on those more basic functions that appear to be threatened nowadays. But the question touches not only anthropology, it is also connected to political issues in a way that

[1] Elizabeth A. Povinelli, *Geontologies: A Requiem to Late Liberalism* (Durham and London: Duke University Press, 2016), 43.
[2] Povinelli, 41.

I would like to expand and focus in the following text. "I can't breathe!" is not only a cry of despair, it is also the political call of movements like *Black Lives Matter* for a world in which breathing should be possible for all; it is part of a "fighting for breathable lives" as Magdalena Górska put it.[3] To hear this cry as a political call means for me not only to change our coexistence and its infrastructures in such a way that everyone can breathe, but also to see in breathing, as in other 'basic' bodily functions, a dimension of freedom that cannot be reduced to the traditional (political) concepts of freedom such as freedom of will or decision. In the following, I would therefore like to work with Povinelli's question in a double transformative sense: as a question that requires rethinking not only anthropology but also the realm of politics in its fundamental notions and tasks.

What I would like to suggest might be named as a 'vegetative' freedom, but more urgent first of all than the question of its naming, is the investigation of the reasons why the dimension of breathing in modern western societies gradually loses relevance to the point of starting to become impossible. In clear contrast, for example, to Asian cultures, in which breathing continues to appear as the fundamental spiritual and vital principle, Western culture is based on a strict separation between freedom and necessity, in which only the first sphere counts, while the second, to which breathing is assigned, is largely faded out and devalued. Giorgio Agamben shows how this hierarchical model can be found already in Aristotle and still informs modern anthropology and physiology. It is, however, only in connection with capitalist modes of production and living conditions that a literally breathless form of embodiment and the devaluation of breathing, as Karl Marx already witnessed, are implemented in the reproduction of western societies with increasingly global effects.

I thus begin with the preliminary question about the reasons for the disappearance of breath, with reference to Agamben, Marx and Achille Mbembe, then move on to Povinelli's analysis of late liberalism, in order to pick up her (transformative) question of where the body is when we look at it from its lungs. I will then present not only Povinelli's response but also discuss Emanuele Coccia's attempt to formulate a contemporary cosmology based on breath. If on the one side Coccia provides a very radical shift of perspective on breath, his ontological approach fails to account for the political dimension of breathing and its differentially distributed possibility. This is why in the last part of my text I will return to political theory and to Frantz Fanon's perspective on the coloniality

---

[3] Magdalena Górska, *Breathing Matters. Feminist Inter-Sectional Politics of Vulnerability*, vol. 683, Linköping Studies in Arts and Science (Linköping University, 2016), 12.

of breathing. As an embodied phenomenon, however, breath cannot be addressed solely by theory. Throughout the text I will also engage with artistic practices experimenting with different modes of sensing and of embodiment. My first reference will be the work of the Karrabing Film Collective that Povinelli is part of and whose films develop a powerful aesthetic that at once displays the destructive effects of extractivist capitalism and unsettles our Western modes of perceiving and creating. My second reference will be to a work by the choreographer and dancer Nora Chipaumire on the visceral impacts of colonialism and racism that I read as developing an embodied mode of resistance reaching down to the dimension of breath. I will conclude with some sketchy reflections on how to conceive of freedom differently if we see breathing as a constitutive dimension of it.

Inside and Outside

Although some of its fundamental concepts (gr. *pneuma*, lat. *spiritus*) derive from breath and ancient Greek cosmologies conceive *pneuma* as the pervading vital principle, breath plays an increasingly marginal or unnoticed role in Western thought.[4] This circumstance is strongly related to the way in which life itself has been conceived in the Western world. At the beginning of his book *The Open,* Giorgio Agamben observes that Western culture never directly determines life: life is "what cannot be defined, yet, precisely for this reason, must be ceaselessly articulated and divided".[5] Emblematic of this analytical procedure is Aristotle's approach in *De anima.* Instead of characterizing life as such, Aristotle divides it into different functions (nutrition, sensation, thought) and concludes that life is to be equated above all with the first, with the so-called vegetative function, since only this one belongs to all living beings. The subdivision of different functions and the comparative view, which characterizes Aristotle's philosophical method, has profound implications. It establishes a clear line of demarcation between the different functions, which then appear as separable from each other. Ancient Greek even has two different terms for life, *bios* and *zoē*,[6] arranged in a hierarchical order of value, mirroring the hierarchy between the different living beings (humans, animals,

---

[4] Górska gives a survey on the rare writings on breath in the 20th and beginning 21st century, cf. Górska, 683:25-28.
[5] Giorgio Agamben, *The Open: Man and Animal* (Stanford University Press, 2004), 13.
[6] Cf. also Giorgio Agamben, *Homo Sacer: Sovereign Power and Bare Life* (Stanford University Press, 1998), 1-12.

plants) that characterizes not only Greek philosophy but also Christian religion. The division of life arising in the ancient and Christian world, continues to inform also modern Western medicine and life sciences. Agamben first traces it to the work of the French anatomist and physiologist Xavier Bichat, who had a strong impact on modern pathology. In his major work *Recherches physiologiques sur la vie et la mort* Bichat distinguishes between a mere organic and an animal life. Organic life, equivalent to Aristotle's vegetative function, includes functions, such as blood circulation, assimilation and excretion, but also breath and these are seen as being *automatically* and *unconsciously* reproduced *inside* the organism. Only life, which he called "animalistic", connects the living being with the *outside* world and is *relationally* conceived by Bichat. In man, he therefore sees two different animals present at the same time—"l'animal existant au-dedans" and "l'animal existant au-dehors" which are not congruent: the former already begins with the foetus, the latter only later in the development of the organism, although it can die earlier than the former.[7] According to Agamben, out of this division of life in a mechanical inside and relational (intelligent) outside, an "obscure background from which the life of the higher animals gets separated"[8] emerges, which he calls "bare life". If this term is problematic in Agamben's political writings because it implies a victimization of those subjects who are described as being reduced to this plane,[9] it is way more intelligible in the medical-biological context in which he first introduces it in *The Open*. Agamben can point there at modern surgery and anaesthesia as practices based on the supposedly clean separability of bodily functions and the respective "animals", as well as discussions on clinical death, as distinguishable from brain death (as defined by Bichat), in order to show the practical reality of this separation.

This very separation between different modalities of life, as it becomes evident in Bichat's formulation, has deep consequences for the Western conception of breath. For according to the functional topology underlying Western philosophy and medicine, breath only belongs to the 'low', automatic and dull functions that serve mere reproduction but not the development and unfolding of life. The obvious relationality of breath therefore disappears from sight behind a mechanical understanding of the

---

[7] Agamben, *The Open*, 14–15.
[8] Agamben, 14.
[9] Since the beginning of the Covid pandemic Agamben also started to use his notion of "bare life" in order to criticize in a very problematic way measures such as green pass or lock-downs. Cf. the open letter of Donatella Di Cesare in the weekly magazine *L'Espresso* for a sharp critique of Agamben's newest comments: Nihil Evadere, "Dear Agamben, Dear Cacciari...", *Contrahistorical* (blog), 31 July 2021, https://medium.com/contrahistorical/dear-agamben-dear-cacciari-fadc2e512f09.

vital (vegetative) functions of the body and thus becomes devalued; the same happens with the vitality and transformative power that breath has in other cultures, such as Hinduism *(prana)* or Daoism *(qi),* when breath is considered a merely unconscious and automatic function.

Breathe so many more Breaths

The mechanization of breath, however, is not solely a product of Western anthropologies, medicine and physiology. It is also socially produced and reproduced. This holds particularly for the capitalist modes of production, beginning with the form of embodiment, labour, that capitalist societies have made into the dominant one and transformed, in order to exploit the body in an unprecedented manner.
In the chapter on the "working day" in the first volume of *Capital,* Karl Marx quotes the London physician Dr. Richardson in order to show the often-deadly implications of capitalist wage labour conditions: "It is not only in dressmakers' rooms that working to death is the order of the day, but in a thousand other places; in every place I had almost said, where 'a thriving business' has to be done […]". Notably, Richardson mentions the impacts on breath as one of the direct effects of the new working conditions:

> The occupation, instinctive almost as a portion of human art, unobjectionable as a branch of human industry, is made by mere excess of work the destroyer of the man. He can strike so many blows per day, walk so many steps, breathe so many breaths, produce so much work, and live an average, say, of fifty years; he is made to strike so many more blows, to walk so many more steps, to breathe so many more breaths per day, and to increase altogether a fourth of his life. He meets the effort; the result is, that producing for a limited time a fourth more work, he dies at 37 for 50.[10]

Like all other activities of life, breath is forced to adapt to the new accelerated work processes in the modern system of wage labour and its "werewolf-like hunger for surplus labour"[11] that does not let up until today. Breath, is thus *made machine-like* because it must conform to

---

[10] Karl Marx, *Capital: A Critique of Political Economy* (Vintage Books, 1977), 366-67.
[11] Marx, 353.

the rhythms and forms of labour, whether in the factory or at computer desks. Breath becomes the unconscious and automatic appendage of the breathless accumulation of capital, the dark background—because it is left in the dark and outside attention—that makes us work.

Although we can thus characterize the capitalist system of production in general as a breathless one, the dictates of capitalist economy also provide an unequal distribution of breath according to gender, class, and race. The cry "I can't breathe!" is connected not only with the increased rhythms, but also with the different architectures and organizations of modern production that for certain groups systematically undermines the possibility of breathing. Factories, mines or polluted cities are in this respect specific sites of an asphyxiating capitalism.

From the advent of capitalism, the shortening of breath, however, did not only concern class division. Marx also provides an early example of the gendered dimension of breathless capitalism, by referring to a sensational headline in the newspapers from 1863: "Death from simple overwork". This sensational, because unprecedented headline denouncing the deadly impact of the new working conditions concerns a woman, Mary Ann Walkley, a 20-year old seamstress, "exploited by a lady with the pleasant name of Elise".[12] In order to get the dresses ready in time for the ball in honour of the new Princess of Wales, Mary Ann worked continuously for 26.5 hours with 30 other women in a small room and slept in close quarters with other workers at night. The doctor certified her death from overwork and from a poorly ventilated sleeping room. Mary Ann suffocated from her working and living conditions, as did many other seamstresses—according to the aforementioned Dr. Richardson—who suffered increasingly from "deficient air, and either deficient food or deficient digestion".[13]

Next to class and gender, the impediment of breath is also connected with racism and antisemitism, as the concentration camps and the asphyxiating acts of racist violence clearly show. Achille Mbembe's notion of "necropolitics" stresses the "work of death" internal to Foucault's concept of biopolitics in form of a "generalized instrumentalization of human existence and the material destruction of human bodies and populations".[14] Although it highlights the "viscerality"[15] of necropolitical technologies and sovereignty it does not analyze the aspect of breathing systematically. Breath is, however, present in many ways throughout

---

[12] Marx, 364.
[13] Marx, 365.
[14] Achille Mbembe, *Necropolitics* (Duke University Press, 2019), 66, 68.
[15] Mbembe, 93.

Mbembe's text, e.g. when he speaks of the use of asphyxiating gases in necropolitical massacres and genocides related to racism and anti-semitism.[16] The impossibility of breathing is also referred to as recurrent outcome of violence inflicted on enslaved bodies.[17] Breath, finally, is also mentioned in relation to Frantz Fanon and to the functioning of "racist fears".[18] What Mbembe highlights here is how racism is fuelled especially by the visceral dimensions of bodies of colour, like breathing or sexuality, that are turned into imaginary forces of aggression and therefore made themselves objects of violent acts. The impossibility of breathing shows therefore to be a direct expression of the economic, biopolitical and necropolitical power and domination that characterizes Western modernity, sovereignty and capitalism since their beginnings. Either because of the lack of air in restricted spaces or the fine dust of the extracted materials, breath is a political site of modernity and its capitalist, colonial and authoritarian dimensions until our days. Capitalism consumes breath, like much else, as a resource taken for granted; as gendered "cheap nature"[19] it exploits it to the point of its fatal extinction.

Becoming Otherwise

Elizabeth Povinelli's work helps to deepen the inquiry into the colonial regime of capitalism. Focusing her anthropological work on the impact of late liberalism on Indigenous groups in the northern territories of Australia, Povinelli points to another and not less devastating division of modern capitalist regimes, the separation of "Life" and "Nonlife", respectively "the difference between the lively and the inert".[20] Accordingly, she argues for a wider frame than the focus on life and death as proposed both by Michel Foucault and Achille Mbembe. Biopolitical and necropolitical analyses are both "hiding and revealing" a broader context where the demarcation and the value of what is considered alive and what is not is at stake.[21] It is a "geontological" divide with epistemic,

---

[16] Mbembe, 61, 120.
[17] Mbembe, 159.
[18] Achille Mbembe, *Necropolitics* (Duke University Press, 2019), 134. I will come back to Fanon in my section on Nora Chipaumire.
[19] Cf. Jason W. Moore, *Capitalism in the Web of Life: Ecology and the Accumulation of Capital* (Verso Books, 2015); Jason W. Moore, "The Capitalocene, Part I: On the Nature and Origins of Our Ecological Crisis", *The Journal of Peasant Studies* 44, no. 3 (4 May 2017): 594–630, https://doi.org/10.1080/03066150.2016.1235036.
[20] Elizabeth A. Povinelli, *Geontologies: A Requiem to Late Liberalism* (Durham and London: Duke University Press, 2016), 4–5.
[21] Povinelli, 4.

political, legal implications, that allowed extractivist and colonialist liberalism to thrive and which manifests itself also in the disciplinary differentiation of and within humanities and natural sciences. "Geontopower", as Povinelli names it, is grounded in a concept of life as "self-oriented sovereignty" supported by the "metabolic function" of its parts (comparable with Bichat's "animal au-dedans"): "The concept of metabolic function", this is how Povinelli characterizes this modern form of life knowledge, which not only applies to the relation organs-body, but also to cells-organs or members-species, "allows us to consider each and every part of the living being as having its own very narrow and contained goals and yet still be part of a living being's broader purpose".[22] The geontological divide and the definition of life as "self-oriented activity"[23] is only possible, according to Povinelli, if life is seen from the perspective of its "final membrane"[24]—in humans or other mammals this is the skin. The final membrane is the place where reproductive processes and regulations take place, i.e. metabolism with the outside. In order for life to appear as a self-oriented activity, a specific "epidermal point of view"[25] is required, which from this outer membrane directs the view primarily into the inside of the organism and thereby fades out or undervalues the interaction with the (Living and Nonliving) outside. At a time, however, when the activities of human "self-oriented sovereignty" have so wreaked havoc on the planet and its carbon cycle, this "epidermal point of view" proves no longer sustainable. Like Donna Haraway, Povinelli therefore questions an epistemic and ethico-political stance that has life end with its skin or some other final membrane and supposedly clear-cut borders. This is also the context in which she formulates the question: "Where is the human body if it is viewed from the lung?".[26] The call to transform one's view not only holds for individuals and their metabolism with the nonliving outside. To look at the body from its lungs also provides a new perspective on the extractivist practices so crucial for the functioning of capitalism. Povinelli depicts this alternative view of human and nonhuman practice with an ink drawing used as front cover of the book and reappearing in its middle, with the title *Breath, 3*.

---

[22] Povinelli, 39.
[23] Povinelli, 39.
[24] Povinelli, 40.
[25] Povinelli, 40.
[26] Cf. Donna Haraway, "A Cyborg Manifesto: Science, Technology, and Socialist-Feminism in the Late Twentieth Century", in *Simians, Cyborgs and Women: The Reinvention of Nature* (London: Routledge, 1991), 178.

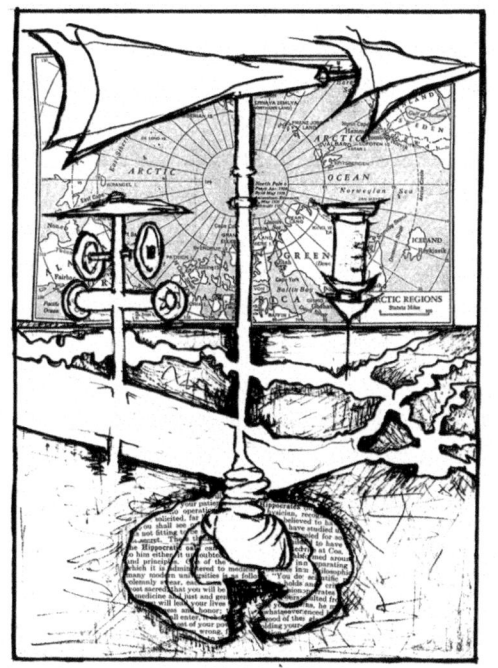

Fig. 1 — Elizabeth A. Povinelli, *Breath, 3,* 2014

The image remains uncommented in the text except from the caption "The politics of breath".[27] Here, if I interpret it correctly, mining and fracking industries are depicted as a toxic metabolism and breathing cycle. Extractive excavations, depicted in form of lungs at the bottom of the image, not only destroy the soil and its surroundings, but also pollute the waters and the air through leaking chemicals and the production of particulate matter, with effects circulating till the Arctic regions, whose map is collaged into the upper half of the drawing, and from there returning in form of climatic change. This toxic "politics of breath", made by the emissions of extraction and combustion, uses the carbon cycle of plants and displaces it at the same time with a deadly one, causing desertification and the pollution of the air. If even capitalism can be described as a breathing cycle, connecting different matters and organisms, technologies and 'natural' sites, this holds even more for breathing bodies. Breath is therefore not only the trace of the geontopower of late liberalism, but serves Povinelli as a concrete phenomenon to challenge and overcome the "abjection of Nonlife",[28] underlying biopolitical as well as necropolitical measures. The "abjection of Nonlife" devalues Indigenous ontologies, that in turn valorize the realm of Nonlife, and drives not only extractivist and (neo-)colonial interests, but also serves the dehumanizing effects of slavery.

Contrary to geontopower, Povinelli tries to think of an entanglement and intertwining of Life and Nonlife, without dramatizing their difference nor simply erasing it. This is what a closer look at breathing reveals: "Animals and minerals, plants and animals, and photoautotrophs and chemoheterotrophs are extimates—each is external to the other only if the scale of our perception is confined to the skin, to a set of epidermal enclosures. But human lungs are constant reminders that this separation is imaginary."[29] Human lungs and respiratory organs in general supply the organism with oxygen (O_2), i.e. Nonlife, in order to be able to burn the nutrients in the cells and thus generate energy for the body. These same respiratory organs then release carbon dioxide (CO_2), which in turn can be used by other metabolisms, such as those of plants. Breath in this view subverts Bichat's topology; reproductive processes like breath make organisms no longer appear as sovereign and self-referential entities, not even as merely relational ones, but as woven into widely ramified entanglements in which the separation of Life and Nonlife as a dichotomous line dissolves or at least becomes obscured. Breath does not merely show the constitutive

---

[27] Elizabeth A. Povinelli, *Geontologies: A Requiem to Late Liberalism* (Durham and London: Duke University Press, 2016), 113.
[28] Povinelli, 44.
[29] Povinelli, 42.

relationality of the living, it shows how Life arises from Nonlife and transforms itself again into Nonlife. The lung and thus the body, in Povinelli's perspective, appears therefore to be "outside [...] as much if not more so than inside".[30] It is a marker of a constant "becoming otherwise"[31] that connects Life and Nonlife once they are no longer regarded through the individualizing lens of western anthropology or the isolating and abstract operations of extractivist interests. This "becoming otherwise" also characterizes the artistic practice and the aesthetics of "improvisational realism"[32] of the Karrabing Film Collective, of which Povinelli is part, together with Indigenous groups from the northern territories of Australia. The films are a collaboration between different people, scientists, artists and activists, all experimenting with a medium they do not master; the group acts and arranges the films entirely by itself; from the first idea of a group member, the film develops different plots, added by the other members of the group and woven together into a new story. "The shots also emerge from the dialogue and much of the setting of each scene of the film is improvised, again based on what people touch, smell, experience, fear, desire. The gap between the realism and the improvisation of the real, neither being reality in any positive sense, allows, I think, for a sudden otherwise to emerge—a sudden seeing or experiencing the infrastructural arrangements of differential existence."[33] The movies are processes of becoming otherwise, where humans become bees, beer cans become musical instruments etc. Through that, while describing different forms of (visceral) colonial violence, they are also an embodiment of fierce resistance and a display of escape-strategies from this very violence. By using Indigenous knowledges and imaginaries, they unsettle the (Western) spectator's view confronting the globalized art places with a not fully seizable experience of Indigenous life. *The Mermaids, or Aiden in Wonderland* (2018) for example, displays the dystopian scenario of a toxic environment, where only Indigenous people can survive "outside"; white people stay "inside"[34] or walk around in huge protective white overalls and face masks, in order to pursue experiments on black lives and extract through and from them resources in "the mud". The plot takes place in the sites and ruins of

---

[30] Povinelli, 100.
[31] Elizabeth A. Povinelli, *Geontologies: A Requiem to Late Liberalism* (Durham and London: Duke University Press, 2016), 137. See also Elizabeth A. Povinelli, "After the Last Man: Images and Ethics of Becoming Otherwise", *e-flux- Journal #35 May 2012*, May 2012, https://www.e-flux.com/journal/35/68380/after-the-last-man-images-and-ethics-of-becoming-otherwise/.
[32] Elizabeth A. Povinelli and Susanne M. Winterling, "Dreams, Nonlinear, Fog, and Breaths", accessed 3 August 2022, https://planetarysensing.com/dreams-nonlinear-fog-and-breaths//.
[33] Povinelli and Winterling.
[34] "Inside" and "outside" are the two first intertitles of the movie.

extractivism: dangerous places protected by the fences of private property, huge fires caused by fracking and water intoxicated by chemicals are the settings in which the different scenes take place, coughing and heavy breathing are repeatedly part of the sound score. The film, like others by the Karrabing Film Collective, does not resolve in the depiction of a damaged world, it also opens up, through the bodies of its performers and a playful and experimental shared use of the technical devices at hand (iPhones), a way out of the suffocating world of late liberalism. The movie appears as a summoning of the powers of Indigenous lands and their sites/dreamings, opening up to an unsettling sequence of images providing an encounter with forces and perceptions that can no longer be rationalized and mastered, as the breathless extractivist and colonial powers continuously try to. The same holds for the last scenes of *Day in The Life* (2020), that in a more documentary mode shows the life in the locked Indigenous camps, the biopolitical policing of the authorities and the polluting traces of mining companies. The film ends with an appeal to the ancestors whose breath (used for playing didgeridoos) dissolves the representatives of authority and mining companies and lets them disappear.

The movies of Karrabing Film Collective enable a multisensorial experience of the violence inflicted by the colonial and capitalist regimes Povinelli writes about in her theoretical analyses. More importantly, however, and with the very same means, they also trigger in the performer as well as in the beholder a becoming otherwise to contrast the phantasm of a "self-oriented sovereignty" Povinelli talks about in her theoretical work. It is the collaborative movie making, therefore, that provides an escape route from the asphyxiating and deadly biopolitical regime inflicted onto Indigenous groups; an unsettling and playful one at the same time.

Jellyfish in the Sea

Emanuele Coccia's treatise *The Life of Plants* follows a different path of critique by challenging many basic assumptions of Western philosophy.[35] Like Povinelli, Coccia opposes an anthropocentric perspective, though unlike her, he does this from what one might call an 'expanded' vitalism that takes neither humans nor animals, but plants as the most disregarded species in Western ontology as starting point. It is through plants, that Coccia approaches breath, which in turn becomes a crucial element of what already in the subtitle of the book is announced as a

---

[35] Emanuele Coccia, *The Life of Plants: A Metaphysics of Mixture,* 1st edition (Medford, MA: Polity, 2018).

Fig. 2 — Karrabing Film Collective, *Mermaids, or Aiden in Wonderland*, still
Courtesy: Elizabeth A. Povinelli

"metaphysics of mixture". Plants interrupt the auto-referentiality of the living by not needing life in order to reproduce: "[t]hey require nothing but the world, nothing but reality in its most basic components: rocks, water, air, light"[36]—i.e. Nonlife. Through their photosynthetic breathing process, plants provide the conditions for breathing for most other living beings.

Despite Coccia's expanded vitalism of plants his position comes quite close to that of Povinelli in seeing breath as entanglement of Life and Nonlife. "To breathe means to be plunged into a medium that penetrates us in the same way and with the same intensity as we penetrate it".[37] For Coccia the circulation of breath also subverts the hierarchy between milieu and individual, as it does with sharp divisions between species: "The air we breathe is not a purely geological or mineral reality—it is not just out there, it is not, as such, an effect of the earth—but rather the breath of other living beings. It is a by-product of 'the lives of others'."[38] Breath is therefore a medium of mixture: "Instead of revealing itself as a space of competition or mutual exclusion, the world opens [...] as the metaphysical space of the most radical form of mixture, the form that makes possible the coexistence of the incompatible, an alchemical laboratory in which everything seems to be able to change its nature, to pass from the organic into the inorganic".[39]

Accordingly, for Coccia, perceiving and thinking through this mixture also means departing from a whole series of dualisms that characterize Western thought and have entangled it in aporia: "The metaphysical space of breath is, above all, contradiction: breathing precedes every distinction between soul *[âme]* and body, between mind *[esprit]* and object, between ideality and reality".[40] The breath thus stands for an intersection of these realms, that does not abolish their differences, but opens them for connections. This has consequences not only for the dualism of soul and body, but also for our understanding of the body itself. Seen from breath and its circulation, the body is not in contact or exchange with its environment as an auto-referential unit, it is fully "immersed" in it.[41] The body is thus not only made of the same 'stuff' as the environment it permeates and which permeates itself; the functional differentiation and inner organization, which Aristotelianism thinks of as an inner hierarchy of the body and its faculties, is also relativized in this perspective:

---

[36] Coccia, 8.
[37] Coccia, 11.
[38] Coccia, 47.
[39] Coccia, 48.
[40] Coccia, 56–57.
[41] Coccia, 31.

So, if being in the world is *immersion,* then thinking and acting, working and breathing, moving, creating, feeling would be inseparable, because an immersed being has a relationship with the world that is not modelled on the relationship that a subject has with an object but on that of a jellyfish with the sea, which allows it to be what it is. There is no material distinction between us and the rest of the world.[42]

Breath is therefore not one of the basic functions of the body, it permeates them all and brings them into connection with each other: "organs are not simply juxtaposed, nor are they materially liquefied into one another. If they constitute *a body,* it is because they share the same *breath*".[43] That which gives the body the unity of "a body" is also that which immersively connects it with its outside, with the other of itself, and interconnects the various activities and inactivities of the body:

> Everything in the realm of the living is the articulation of breath: from perception to digestion, from thought to pleasure, from speech to locomotion. Everything is a repetition, intensification, and variation of what takes place in breath. [...] What we call life is only this gesture, through which a portion of matter distinguishes itself from the world with the same force that it uses to merge with it.[44]

The body, seen from its breath, thus becomes fluid and rhythmically connected to its environment. It becomes, in Deleuze and Guattari's words, a "body without organs"[45]: the breath subverts the functional distinction so important to Aristotelianism and the internal topology to which it subjects the body. Breath is not a function of the body next to others, but the intersection and opening of these functions for each other as well as for an exchange with the world, which can be reception or elimination, permeability, but also resistance. Infused with breath, the various functions are not simply juxtaposed and subject to a strict division of labour, they interpenetrate and merge. The immateriality, or as Coccia says, the "insubstantiality"[46] of breath is the medium of this intermingling and transformation of a body (dealing) with the world.

---

[42] Coccia, 32.
[43] Coccia, 51–52.
[44] Coccia, 55–56.
[45] Gilles Deleuze and Felix Guattari, "November 28, 1947: How Do You Make Yourself a Body Without Organs?", in A Thousand Plateaus: Capitalism and Schizophrenia, 2nd edition (Minneapolis: University of Minnesota Press, 1987), 149–66.
[46] Coccia, *The Life of Plants,* 55.

Coccia explains the aspect of immersion, which in the last years has become rather popular in the visual arts,[47] primarily by using the example of music. According to Coccia, music allows us to experience the world "as something composed not of objects but of fluxes that pass through us and that we ourselves enter, of waves of variable intensity and in permanent movement".[48] Similarly, Deleuze and Guattari had already assigned music a special role with the figure of the refrain in *A Thousand Plateaus*.[49] Music affects because its rhythms and modulations make it possible to consciously experience the currents and intensities in which the spatiality and temporality of the world are shaped, and at the same time also propose new rhythms and temporalities. The club, in whose darkened rooms the eyes lose importance and in which music acquires the most pervasive effect possible thus becomes an ontologically important place for Coccia, since "it allows us to seize the deepest structure of the world, one that the eyes, at times, prevent us from perceiving".[50]

Coccia's book is a metaphysical treaty of a peculiar kind. It is not a work on the most abstract categories or first principles of being, but a form, as I might call it, of 'sensuous knowledge' in which engaging with the life of plants or with music and clubs not only challenges basic assumptions of Western ontology, like anthropocentrism, but aims at enabling new perceptions and awareness of entanglements. In one aspect, however, it uncritically sticks with a familiar gesture of Western metaphysics: it fully excludes political and social issues from its sight. Unlike Povinelli, Coccia nowhere speaks of how political and economic conditions shape and change the mixture he sees as ontologically fundamental, or interrupt it even by way of constructing borders. Talking of everything being connected to everything through breath fails to recognize, as Haraway captures it in contrast that "everything is connected to something",[51] and that this connection can be politically disrupted, colonized, expropriated. Accordingly also the possibility of breath can be politically regulated and

---

[47] For example, the Berliner Festspiele's program series "Immersion" under the artistic direction of Thomas Oberender (2016-2021), has gathered different formats and contributions from artists "who transcended the conventional oppositions between work and viewer, stage and auditorium, object and observer" and "also aimed to articulate and establish "immersion" as a key term for a different understanding of the world" (Berliner Festspiele, "Immersion—Immersion", accessed 3 August 2022, https://www.berlinerfestspiele.de/en/immersion/start.html.)

[48] Coccia, *The Life of Plants*, 31.

[49] Gilles Deleuze and Felix Guattari, "1837: Of the Refrain", in *A Thousand Plateaus: Capitalism and Schizophrenia*, 2nd edition (Minneapolis: University of Minnesota Press, 1987), 310–50.

[50] Coccia, *The Life of Plants*, 33.

[51] Donna J. Haraway, *Staying with the Trouble: Making Kin in the Chthulucene (Experimental Futures)* (Duke University Press Books, 2016), 31.

unequally distributed, so that a hierarchy between ontology and politics, as Coccia implicitly retains it, is no longer tenable.

Just as the reference to music can direct the view to various rhythms and modulations of breath, a political perspective is at odds with the harmonic mixture that Coccia's ontology presents, thus betraying a specific (Western) positionality. In order to address these issues, another form of sensuous knowledge is needed, one that accounts for the experiences of discrimination and embodied violence cutting or reducing the possibility of breathing, but also displaying and supporting opposition against it on the same embodied level.

Sonic Resistance

In *Black Skin, White Masks,* Frantz Fanon vividly describes how racism, colonialism and sexism not only work on a discursive or categorial level, but invade and divide the body schema of the colonized. In this text too, but in a very different way, breath plays an important role, being the site where colonial domination through shocks, fear, and constriction makes itself felt as an "impossibility of expansion".[52] As Ziauddin Sardar notes in his 2008 preface, throughout Fanon's text one hears the gasps, the visceral suffocation that racism and colonialism provide not only through direct physical violence, but through discriminatory attributions and social discrimination.[53]

In *The Wretched of the Earth* the dimension of breath performatively sounds through the pages, but it is in *A Dying Colonialism* and more precisely in the first chapter "Algeria Unveiled" on the resistance of Algerian women that Fanon pinpoints the relation of breathing and colonialism, while he at the same time reveals breathing as a site of resistance: "There is not occupation of territory, on the one hand, and independence of persons on the other. It is the country as a whole, its history, its daily pulsation that are contested, disfigured, in the hope of a final destruction. Under these conditions, the individual's breathing is an observed, an occupied breathing. It is a combat breathing".[54] Fanon touches on a

---

[52] Frantz Fanon, *Black Skin, White Masks* (London: Pluto Press, 1986), 17.
[53] Fanon, xii.
[54] Frantz Fanon, *A Dying Colonialism,* trans. Haakon Chevalier (Grove Press, 1967), 65. I became aware of this passage through the work of Shahram Khosravi, who gave a lecture entitled "Combat Breathing" within the international program series "Bodies, un-protected", organized by Sandra Noeth and Anna Wagner, at Mousonturm, Frankfurt a.M., in November 2020. Shahram Khosravi, "Künstlerhaus Mousonturm—Shahram Khosravi Combat Breathing", accessed 16 January 2022, https://www.mousonturm.de/events/breath-lecture/.

Fig. 3 — Nora Chipaumire, *portrait of myself as my father,*
Photo: Galen Fletcher, Walker Art Centre, 2018

very important point here, although he does not inquire further into it. I would therefore like to give more flesh to his notion of "combat breathing" by referring to a work from performing arts and notably of dance, as a medium able to display but also to transform visceral dimensions of the body.

Nora Chipaumire's piece *portrait of myself as my ~~father~~,* that premiered in 2016, can be seen as setting up a scene of combat breathing since the piece literally takes place within a boxing ring and provides, at least in a crucial scene of the piece, a very sonic and choreographic experience of breath. Throughout the piece Chipaumire and Senegalese dancer Pape Ibrahima Ndiaye (a.k.a. Kaolack), embodying an imaginary daughter and father, are tied together in an energetic and exhausting dance, accompanied by New York dancer Shamar Wayne Watt, in the roles of coach, corner man, cheerleader, shadow. The piece is a very personal work, in which Chipaumire engages with the spectre of the absent father she lost as a child, envisioning him as an idealized figure using sport as a point of entrance, but also putting his stereotypical masculinity under pressure. As many of Chipaumire's choreographies, also this one works itself through stereotypes, as forms of simplified and rigid determinations imposed on individuals and groups by way of discriminatory practices and discourses; it tries to lay bare what is often largely retained unconsciously, but produces massive bodily effects, by limiting and determining not only the appearance but also the scope of action including visceral processes like breathing.

Sport, dance, choreography and voice are the means Chipaumire uses to show stereotypes and limitations and at the same time to engage with modes of embodied resistance and transformative practice. As the artist puts it: "I'm interested in all that a body can do which means also its sonic production as well as its physical gesture".[55] In a crucial scene from *portrait of myself as my ~~father~~,* the sonic and the physical come together in an intense sequence of what Chipaumire calls "A Black Manifesto". The scene is a loud interrogation of the imaginary father figure, standing for all black men, by Chipaumire. As Chipaumire puts it in her own commentary, the sequence combines elements of a hazing with those of a ritual process of transformation.[56] Kaolack's movements alternate between kneeling down, rising up, stepping/running in different directions

---

[55] BatesDanceFestival, "Artist Proflie Nora Chipaumire 2018", 2018, https://www.youtube.com/watch?v=KFA-Mg6zHsA.

[56] The whole scene can be seen here (with a commentary of the artist): BAMorg, "A Closer Look: Nora Chipaumire on Portrait of Myself as My Father", 2020, https://www.youtube.com/watch?v=3M4SuEy6r6w.

with the arms reaching out, in an accelerating rhythm that is fired up by Chipaumire's voice. The scene touches upon different layers, the relationship between a daughter and an absent father, of past and future, of black masculinity and humanity, but within the overall frame of liberation struggles. Chipaumire asks different questions such as, "What time is it Black?" or "Black, am I a man Black?" and ends with the statement "Black, it's time, Black is time, it is Black time". She therefore characterizies the whole sequence as a process of transformation and liberation. In the end Kaolack is lying on the floor, contracting their muscles and releasing down, as a moment of breakthrough and transformation.

Although one does not immediately notice it, breath is very present in Chipaumire's interrogation—amplified and rendered spacious by the microphone—and in Kaolack's answers. Pictures cannot catch this dimension that accompanies speech, but also exceeds it; they can at best display the physicality of the breath/voice, it's taking place and space within in the body.

If you start paying attention to it, breath does not only accompany voice and movement as it usually does. The scene presents different modulations of breath, expressive of the different stages the figures are in, so that the whole scene can be read as a process of reclaiming breath and of also liberating the breath through dance, voice and movement. The sequence begins with loud and restless breathing, related to a condition of constriction, of fear and even fugitiveness. During the course of the scene and together with the process of questioning, the breath deepens and changes its rhythm. The questioning provides an inward movement and also marks the steps of a process of rising awareness and liberation by shifting the meaning of Blackness. Kaolack's body first engages in a series of fractured and spasmodic movements that recall gestures of fright or even of flight. Through the voice and the movement of the other bodies on stage, it gets more involved into an intensified and continuous movement, reaching a trance-like intensity, after which it lays on the floor twitching. As Chipaumire's vocalization during the hazing/initiation becomes calmer and deeper, Kaolack's body appears to be coming into a state where, after intense movements, they are not only (automatically) catching, but also actively reconquering their breath. His shrugging movements on the floor are the modulations of a process of disrupting the restricting and discriminatory sedimentations within the Black body, that as Fanon shows essentially sit in the lungs.

As also Mbembe states, dance and song are ways through which "the colonized restructure their perception", and this, one might add with respect to Chipaumire's sequence, because they materially and effectively allow the body to regain and be pervaded by breath.[57] Again, with reference to Fanon, Mbembe highlights how "liberation, decolonization, [...] changing the world order, the upsurge, exiting the great night [...] is not spontaneous [...] it has as specific rhythm".[58] The process through which the entangled bodies on stage undergo a process of transformation is a rhythmic one, provided by a continuous crescendo, that does not provide an immersion into the world, as in Coccia's club, but an "exiting" from an oppressive one, by a wrangling and displacement of the gendered bodies and a breaking free from visceral violence. In describing the struggle for liberation within Fanon's writing, Mbembe provides a description that seems to describe the movement of Chipaumire's choreography: "It engages with everything: muscles, bare fists, intelligence, the suffering from which one is not spared, blood. A new gesture, it creates new respiratory rhythms. The Fanonian fighter is a human who breathes anew, whose muscular tensions unclench, and whose imagination is in celebration."[59] Chipaumire's scene uses voice and dance as primary means in this visceral struggle for breath. "Through live art", Chipaumire says, "we are afforded the opportunity to study everything that makes us human, everything".[60] Fanon's "combat breathing" could be a very useful formula for describing what performance art can do, maybe even more impressively than video, in that it displays how breath is a contested place and at the same time shows ways through which it can be recaptured, fought for and collectively transformed. It is in this sense that the sequence appears to be a dance of reclaiming breath, of liberating the bodies through movement and voice, through a moving together that escapes the suffocating impact of stereotypes and resists visceral colonial domination.

Another Freedom

Whenever performance and dance engage in energetic movements, breath becomes more audible. If breath first goes unnoticed in Chipaumire's performance, even though it is emphasized in its materiality, it is because our attention is so often focused on words or movements. With my reference to different theoretical and artistic practices, I wanted to shed light and engage in a sensuous investigation of where a body is, but also what a body does and can do, when addressed in and through its breath.

[57] Mbembe, *Necropolitics,* 141.
[58] Mbembe, 140.
[59] Mbembe, 141.
[60] BatesDanceFestival, "Artist Profile Nora Chipaumire 2018".

The ongoing pandemic has focused the attention on breathing in unprecedented ways. As SARS-CoV-2 infects the lungs and spreads through the air we breathe, breathing and especially breathing together has become a topic. Face masks shorten the breath and make it sound louder, by filtering the air we commonly breathe and trying to protect us from infecting one another. In this way, the pandemic provides an experience of the materiality of breathing and at the same time, by preventing us breathing the same air it cuts through the social tissue, it undermines mixture and contact, it separates us.

Coccia writes, that "[w]e reach out as far as our breath does"; the pandemic gives a collective experience of how restricted and unfree we become when our breath cannot reach out, reach for the others and become immersed in the same airy matter. The no doubt necessary measure of wearing masks not only shortens breath, and in doing so increases anxiety, it restricts movements and slows down or even diminishes public space. In this deeply transformed social environment the pandemic, paradoxically, exposes those groups more strongly to contagion, who in pre-pandemic times were the ones more suffocated by toxic environments or social control because they are less provided with the means to protect themselves (houses, face masks, medical care etc.).

The films of the Karrabing Film Collective and the performance of Nora Chipaumire are different ways of using artistic means to highlight and criticize toxic or racist politics of breathing, but at the same time to create spaces (in and outside the bodies) in which breathing becomes possible in a different way. They thereby make clear that freedom starts in these visceral and material realms. An understanding of freedom that equates it only to action, will and decision falls short, because it fails to acknowledge the living conditions of these activities. Reaching down to these conditions means to touch the point where freedom is connected to necessity and inseparable from it. Breath accompanies life in all its expressions and forms; it goes by itself, without one having to want it, but at the same time it is also malleable and changeable. Breath can change its rhythm, breath is not individual but shared, and this across species, as Coccia points out, as well as across the separation of Life and Nonlife, as Povinelli highlights. Breath is dependent on other people, on viruses, on air and water, and therefore fragile; but it is also a site of resistance and struggle, it can be reclaimed and reconquered, even in the controlled enclaves of (neo-)colonialism domination. Breath allows us to think matter and materiality not as solid, but as rhythmic, as going with rhythms, and producing rhythms, in connection with others and with the otherwise.

To think breath as a cipher for freedom, to think a freedom of breath, means to think freedom and necessity, freedom and dependence together, and therefore also to fight for our dependencies, dependencies on other bodies, on infrastructures, on plants and oxygen, on non-acidic seas and freezing regions. Breath connects our visceral interiors to the diversity of a living and inert outside. So paying attention to breath is perhaps the simplest way to experience that freedom is not sovereignty, but an uncontrollable and shared power.

References

Agamben, Giorgio. *Homo Sacer: Sovereign Power and Bare Life.* Stanford University Press, 1998.

——— *The Open: Man and Animal.* Stanford University Press, 2004.

BAMorg. *A Closer Look: Nora Chipaumire on Portrait of Myself as My Father,* 2020. https://www.youtube.com/watch?v=3M4SuEy6r6w.

BatesDanceFestival. *Artist Profile Nora Chipaumire 2018,* 2018. https://www.youtube.com/watch?v=KFA-Mg6zHsA.

Coccia, Emanuele. *The Life of Plants: A Metaphysics of Mixture.* 1st edition. Medford, MA: Polity, 2018.

Deleuze, Gilles, and Felix Guattari. "1837: Of the Refrain". In *A Thousand Plateaus: Capitalism and Schizophrenia,* 2nd edition., 310–50. Minneapolis: University of Minnesota Press, 1987.

——— "November 28, 1947: How Do You Make Yourself a Body Without Organs?" In *A Thousand Plateaus: Capitalism and Schizophrenia,* 2nd edition., 149–66. Minneapolis: University of Minnesota Press, 1987.

Evadere, Nihil. "Dear Agamben, Dear Cacciari...". *Contrahistorical* (blog), 31 July 2021. https://medium.com/contrahistorical/dear-agamben-dear-cacciari-fadc2e512f09.

Fanon, Frantz. *A Dying Colonialism.* Translated by Haakon Chevalier. Grove Press, 1967.

——— *Black Skin, White Masks.* London: Pluto Press, 1986.

Festspiele, Berliner. "Immersion—Immersion". Accessed 3 August 2022. https://www.berlinerfestspiele.de/en/immersion/start.html.

Haraway, Donna J. "A Cyborg Manifesto: Science, Technology, and Socialist-Feminism in the Late Twentieth Century". In *Simians, Cyborgs and Women: The Reinvention of Nature,* 149–81. London: Routledge, 1991.

——— *Staying with the Trouble: Making Kin in the Chthulucene (Experimental Futures).* Duke University Press Books, 2016.

Khosravi, Shahram. "Künstlerhaus Mousonturm—Shahram Khosravi Combat Breathing". Accessed 16 January 2022. https://www.mousonturm.de/events/breath-lecture/.

Magdalena Górska. *Breathing Matters. Feminist Inter-Sectional Politics of Vulnerability.* Vol. 683. Linköping Studies in Arts and Science. Linköping University, 2016.

Marx, Karl. *Capital: A Critique of Political Economy.* Vintage Books, 1977.

Mbembe, Achille. *Necropolitics.* Duke University Press, 2019.

Moore, Jason W. *Capitalism in the Web of Life: Ecology and the Accumulation of Capital.* Verso Books, 2015.

——— "The Capitalocene, Part I: On the Nature and Origins of Our Ecological Crisis". *The Journal of Peasant Studies* 44, no. 3 (4 May 2017): 594–630. https://doi.org/10.1080/03066150.2016.1235036.

Povinelli, Elizabeth A. "After the Last Man: Images and Ethics of Becoming Otherwise", e-Flux Journal #35 May 2012, May 2012. https://www.e-flux.com/journal/35/68380/after-the-last-man-images-and-ethics-of-becoming-otherwise/.

――― *Geontologies: A Requiem to Late Liberalism.* Durham and London: Duke University Press, 2016.

Povinelli, Elizabeth A., and Susanne M. Winterling. "Dreams, Nonlinear, Fog, and Breaths". Accessed 3 August 2022. https://planetarysensing.com/dreams-nonlinear-fog-and-breaths/.

Basel Abbas and Ruanne Abou-Rahme
Being in the Negative

Our way of thinking about breath and breathing goes back a long way, and refers to the impossibility of the Palestinian condition, in the sense that you are aware, from a very young age, that your very presence is questioned, that you should not even exist. So it's not just that you're in danger at any given moment when you are in Palestine. Yes, you are in danger, but also there is this constant narrative that is material, infrastructural—through the system of occupation, of colonization, of apartheid—that is basically all about negating you entirely. This negation is what we're trying to get to: where the breath is not just a physical breath, but also an existential question, especially if you are a people who 'shouldn't exist', or one who 'doesn't exist'. As a child, I remember more than once, when I was asked where I am from and I'd say I'm from Palestine, I'd be told that there was no such thing as Palestine or Palestinians.

Of course there are physical dimensions; as we all know, you could be shot, you could be maimed, you could get choked from the teargas… But there's also a much deeper question, which is a question of being. Because you're in this continual state of precarity, you have this constant sense that you don't actually exist. This idea of breathing where you should not be able to breathe is also a question of continuing to be, continuing to claim yourself, to claim space and to claim narrative, to claim your story and your testimony. We started thinking a lot about how to exist, then, in these impossible conditions. What are the tools that we can use not just to survive, but also to generate different possibilities?

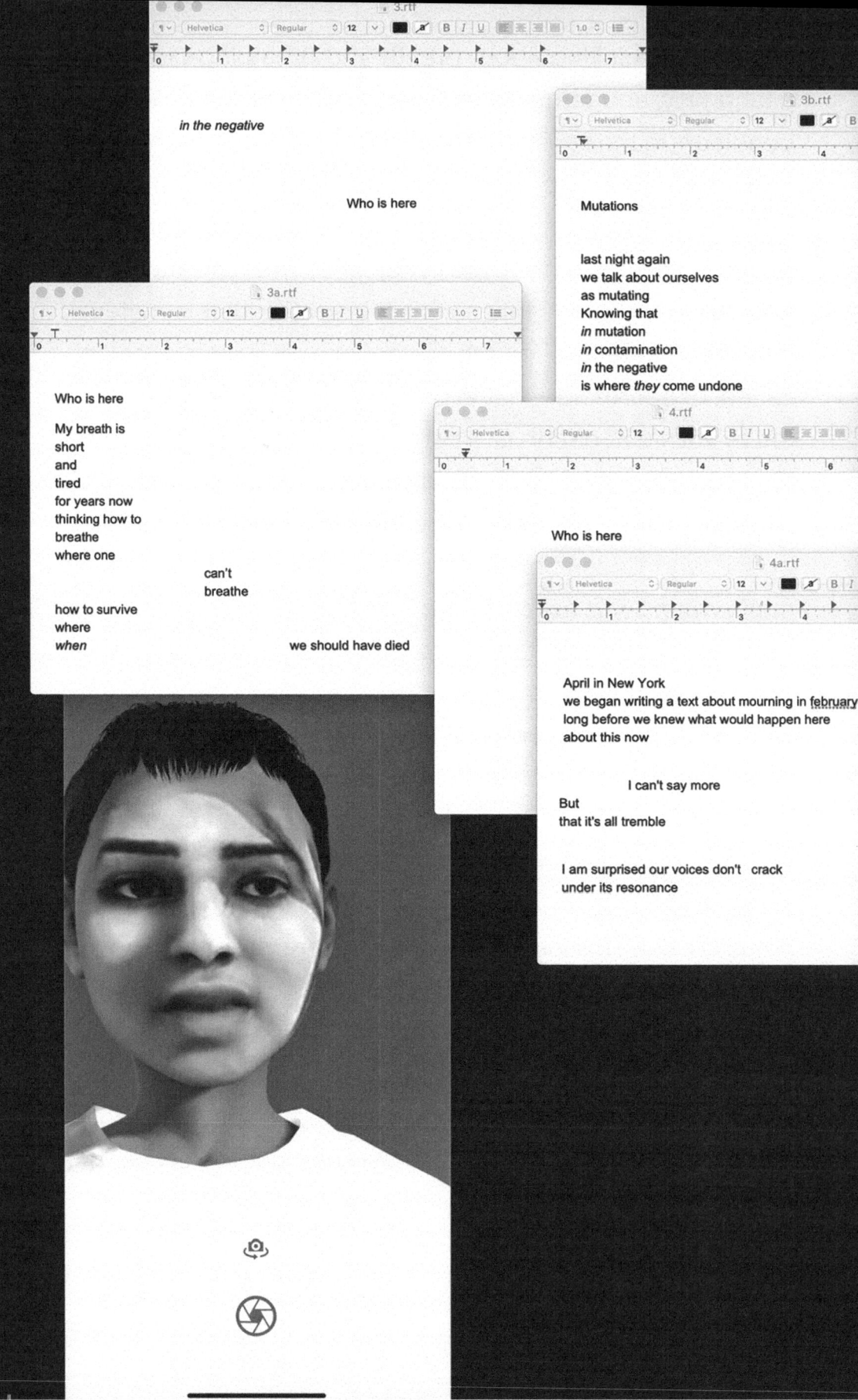

16:51

Gradient

In that sense, the idea of the mask, as well as Adrienne Rich's poem, became very important for us. In the poem, she's underwater and losing consciousness, and it's her scuba-diving mask that gives her life and gives her power—power to be in a space where she shouldn't be, and to breathe when she shouldn't be able to breathe anymore.

It's a question of how to continue, how to mutate, in order to survive in conditions where you should have already died, whether physically or through all kinds of forms of slow violences. That's why Edward Said's text was so interesting for us, because he talks about it. He doesn't say mutation, he says something like, "How easily we change, and are changed". For us, the question was: How can you think of these conditions not just as negative outcomes, but as the very tools from which you create and become unbound from colonial capture, conditions, and time? So you embrace the idea of being inside something that's broken, and move away from the idea of a politics of wanting to fix that thing—or of wanting for it to be recognized as something that is happening to you. It's a question of how to be in the thing that's lacking, how to be in the negative and in the loss, and how to create different possibilities of being and breathing.

In our work *At those terrifying frontiers where the existence and disappearance of people fade into each other,* fragments from Edward Said's most personal and poetic work *After the Last Sky* are repurposed to create a new script that reflects on what it means now to be constructed as an 'illegal' person, body or entity. The script is turned into a song sung and performed by us as multiple avatars. Using a software that generates avatars from a single image, the avatars in the video are all drawn from people who participated in the March of Return, that continues to take place on the seamline in Gaza, an area that has been under physical siege by the Israeli army since 2006. With the impossibility of us, while being only 100 km away in Palestine, of reaching the marchers and of the marchers reaching us, the avatars that are created create a composite between the original images and us as the performers of the avatars. The work attempts to rupture this impossible imposed distance in an act of intense proximity and new becoming. The algorithm in the avatar software renders the missing data and information (due to the low resolution of images circulated online) in the original image as scars, glitches, and incomplete features on the avatar's faces. By keeping and not 'fixing' these visible scars, the work speaks not only to the violence of the material reality but also to the often invisible and embedded violence of representation itself in the circulation/consumption of images and, ultimately, to the violence in the algorithm. *At those terrifying frontiers* thinks about how to continue, how to mutate, in order to not just survive but to generate resistant possibilities of being and breathing within impossible conditions of violence and erasure.

Edited extract from "Being in the Negative", https://perpetualpostponement.org/being-in-the-negativean-interview-with-basel-abbas-and-ruanne-abou-rahme/

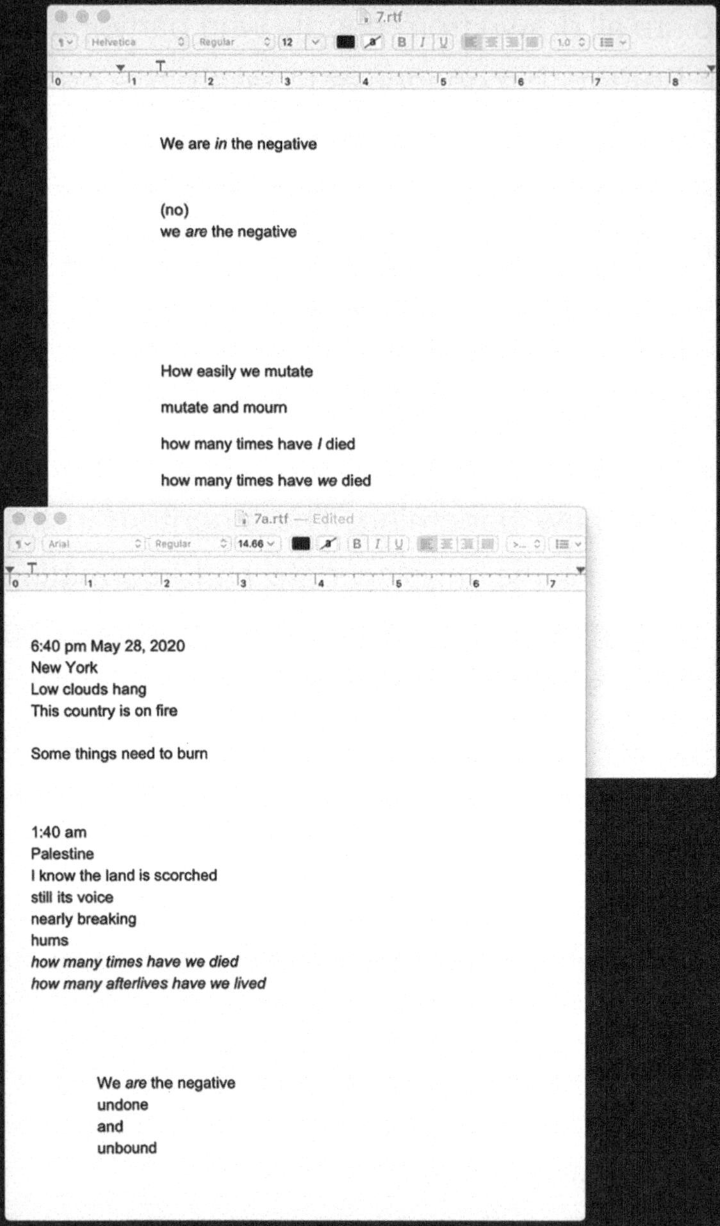

We are *in* the negative

(no)
we *are* the negative

How easily we mutate

mutate and mourn

how many times have *I* died

how many times have *we* died

6:40 pm May 28, 2020
New York
Low clouds hang
This country is on fire

Some things need to burn

1:40 am
Palestine
I know the land is scorched
still its voice
nearly breaking
hums
how many times have we died
how many afterlives have we lived

    We *are* the negative
    undone
    and
    unbound

Shahram Khosravi

The Archive of Stolen Breaths

Our world is a suffocating world. The colour line which is always also a class line is based on the differential distribution of the right to breathe. There are many who cannot breathe; the illegalized people on the move who are suffocated to death in crowded containers; travellers without papers who drown in the Mediterranean Sea; African Americans who are asphyxiated to death under the knees of a brutal racism; people for whom breathing has become a struggle due to the toxic air; and nations who live under imperial conditions such as for the Iranian people who suffer under USA-led sanctions. In such a suffocating world the atmospheric relations are shaped in a way that has turned breathing (literally and figuratively) into a combat. As Frantz Fanon puts it:

> There is not occupation of territory, on the one hand, and independence of persons on the other. It is the country as a whole, its history, its daily pulsation that are contested, disfigured, in the hope of a final destruction. Under these conditions, the individual's breathing is an observed, an occupied breathing. It is a combat breathing.[1]

Sixty years after Fanon wrote these lines the current pandemic crisis has displayed more explicitly than ever how life itself has become the main agenda of

[1] Frantz Fanon, *A Dying Colonialism,* trans. Haakon Chevalier (Grove Press, 1967), 50.

the politics in the modern age. The politics of life turns human biology and breathing into a central issue for the political order. Breathing has become not only a vital bodily function but also a political concern. Breathing has become a political urgency that reveals unequal distributions of life chances organized through a convergence of race and class. The fact that breathing has become a differentially distributed right, makes breathing a political issue. Following several traces of breathlessness across time and space I want to illuminate the political vulnerabilities of certain bodies. The concept of *stolen breaths* brings together various forms of the—slow or quick—violence, that individuals or groups are exposed to.

Toxic Atmospherics

The day I started to write this essay in early January 2022, Baktash Abtin, a dissident Iranian poet and filmmaker passed away in a prison in Tehran after contracting COVID-19. The authorities denied him medical assistance when he first showed symptoms of the disease a month earlier. The coronavirus causes lungs infection and disruption of lung function leading to breathing difficulty. The prison authorities exposed the poet to death by letting the virus do its job properly, of taking over all of the lungs. He struggled to breathe and after several weeks, all the air left his body. An elegy written for him by Shams Langeroodi, a well-known Iranian poet, starts this way:[2]

>Your air has been stolen from you[2]

In October 2019 Essex police discovered 39 undocumented Vietnamese migrants who had suffocated to death in a truck. They had started their journey in the truck in Belgium in the hope of finding a future in the UK. One of them was Pham Thi Tra My, a 26 year old

[2] https://www.youtube.com/watch?v=pSfK07kzdHI, accessed 17/3/2022.

woman who documented the final moments of her life in a text message to her mother:

> I'm sorry Mum. My journey abroad hasn't succeeded.
> Mum, I love you so much!
> I'm dying because I can't breathe.

<u>Documented</u> cases show that during 2021 more than 3000 people died attempting to reach Europe by sea.³ This is an average of eight persons per day.

> Eight persons today.
> Eight persons tomorrow.
> Eight persons the day after tomorrow.
> Eight persons the day after the day after tomorrow.

Drowning is a form of death by suffocation. The lungs take in water and oxygen stops being delivered to the heart. The average person can hold their breath for around 30 seconds. For children, the duration is even shorter. After that they sink. Breathless.

<u>How</u> many times can a Black throat pressed under a white knee repeat "I can't breathe" before he or she stops breathing?

<u>11</u> times Eric Garner repeated "I can't breathe" before dying in New York City on 17 July 2014.
<u>12</u> times David Dungay Jr an Aboriginal Australian man repeated "I can't breathe" before dying in New South Wales Corrective Services custody at the Long Bay Correctional Centre, on 29 September 2015.
<u>17</u> times Byron Williams repeated "I can't breathe" before dying on 5 September 2019 in Las Vegas.
<u>27</u> times George Floyd repeated "I can't breathe" before dying in Minneapolis on 25 May 2020.

---

³ Andrea Garcia Borja et al., "Deaths on Maritime Migration Routes to Europe Soar in First Half of 2021: IOM Brief", International Organization for Migration, 14 July 2021, https://www.iom.int/news/deaths-maritime-migration-routes-europe-soar-first-half-2021-iom-brief.

Twenty-seven times

I can't breathe   I can't breathe   I   can't

breathe   I can't breathe   I can't breathe I

can't breathe   I can't breathe   I   can't

breathe   I can't breathe   I can't breathe I

can't breathe   I can't breathe   I   can't

breathe   I can't breathe   I can't breathe

I can't breathe   I can't breathe I can't

breathe   I can't breathe I can't breathe

I   can't   breathe   I can't   breathe

I can't   breathe I   can't

breathe   I can't breathe   I

can't   breathe   I can't breathe

"I can't breathe!" is a statement. Rather than an appeal for life, it is an allegation against racism and white supremacy. It is a refusal of the conditions that negate Black life.[4] It declares that one's breath is stolen. The list of Black people who have died in the American law enforcement custody after saying the three words "I can't breathe" has reached seventy.[5] These are only the documented cases.

"We are suffocating. There is no air here", Shaheen told me in late December 2021. He is a middle-aged man who works as a vendor in Tehran where the heavily polluted air has turned breathing into a daily struggle. One of the factors that has contributed to the deterioration of air quality in large cities in Iran has been the decades-long sanctions against Iran. While Iranian refineries produce more than half a million barrels of mazut per day, the sanction has stopped its export. So the Iranian authorities use the mazut in power plants. Mazut is a low-quality fossil fuel which is a 'leftover' from refineries. Burning it releases high-level sulphur dioxide emissions. On average Tehrani people have one clean day per month. The official sources show that air pollution causes more than 5000 premature deaths every year. It is also the main cause of increase in diseases such as lung cancer and asthma. The fact that Shaheen has to work on the streets every day exposes him to more toxic air than others who can stay and work in indoor spaces equipped with air filtration systems. He is entitled to breathe clean air only once every 29 days. That is a question of environmental justice and unequal distribution of the right to breath. A consequence of the international sanctions is weaponization of atmospherics, which targets less privileged groups.

---

[4] Ashton T. Crawley, *Blackpentecostal Breath* (New York: Fordham University Press, 2017), 1.
[5] Mike Baker et al., "Three Words. 70 Cases. The Tragic History of 'I Can't Breathe.'", *The New York Times,* 29 June 2020, sec. U.S., https://www.nytimes.com/interactive/2020/06/28/us/i-cant-breathe-police-arrest.html.

In mid-November 2021, a peaceful protest was started by poor farmers in the city of Isfahan in central Iran. For weeks they organized a sit-in protest against water shortages on the dry Zayadneh-rud riverbed that crosses the central city. Thousands of other citizens joined them in the dry riverbed to raise objections against the diversion of water from the Zayadneh-rud river through huge pipelines to other regions and industrial complexes. The water has been transferred to the huge industries which surrounds the city such as the steel factories, which are largest in the Middle East while farmers have been pushed towards the verge of bankruptcy. Moreover, these industries have turned Isfahan into the most polluted city in the country. One of the slogans by the protesters was:

Give Isfahan a chance to breathe!

The peaceful protests of the farmers demanding water and clean air were confronted with violent reaction by the security forces who opened fire and used tear gas. Tear gas is a chemical weapon which infiltrates the lungs through the nose and mouth to cause chest pain and breathlessness. It turns the air you inhale into a weapon against you.
Tear gas has been vastly been deployed in turning the air into a weapon in the service of the states. Making breathing difficult and making the atmosphere suffocating has been a recurrent state tactic against any dissident political interventions. Using tear gas has become a normalized technique in controlling and pushing back people when the state order of bodies and voices is interrupted by "those who have no right to be counted as speaking beings make themselves of some account".[6] From a colonial practice against Indigenous nationals and the oppression of protesters in Iran, to the violent push back of refugees along European borders, tear gas is the weapon that takes away

---

[6] Jacques Rancière, *Disagreement: Politics and Philosophy,* trans. Julie Rose (Minneapolis: University of Min-nesota Press, 1999), 27.

the breath, and thereby to removes bodies and stifles voices.

Tear gas not only steals away breath, but it also shrinks the social air. By taking breath away, tear gas makes the speech and demands of protesting bodies on the streets difficult. The verb 'to stifle' means both to suffocate and to silence. Strangling and silencing are semantically related. Controlling people's breathing is a way to control their speech. Controlling breathing and thereby controlling voices is made possible through the shrinking of social air.[7]

Christina Sharpe uses "the weather" as a metaphor for showing how the anti-Blackness has become pervasive as a climate and is part of the atmospheric relations that makes breathing impossible for Black people. From the bodies of Black people discarded in the ocean from slave ships to the body of George Floyd, Christina Sharpe sees breathlessness as "weather" that always accompanies Black life from the Middle Passage across the Atlantic and beyond.[8]

In another context, Umut Yildirim uses "breathing methodology" to articulate theories of subjugation and violence against human and non-human life and politics within the context of environmental degradation, genocide, and colonial occupation in Kurdistan.[9] Similarly, Kristen Simmons observes that settler atmospherics are the violence which structure colonial practices.

> The conditions we breathe in are collective and unequally distributed, with particular qualities and intensities that are felt differently through and across time. For Indigenous nations, the imbrications of U.S. militarism, industrialism, and

---

[7] Gabriel O. Apata, "'I Can't Breathe': The Suffocating Nature of Racism", *Theory, Culture & Society* 37, no. 7–8 (1 December 2020): 241–54, https://doi.org/10.1177/0263276420957718.

[8] Christina Sharpe, *In the Wake: On Blackness and Being* (Durham, NC: Duke University Press, 2016), https://doi.org/10.1215/9780822373452.

[9] Umut Yildirim, "Breathing under Blockade: Displaced and Diasporic Ecologies in a Middle Eastern Heritage Site", *Current Anthropology,* Forthcoming.

capitalism have always been palpably felt on Indigenous lands and through Indigenous bodies, from extraction to experimentation. The regimes of this foundational violence are the surrounds of settler atmospherics.[10]

The atmosphere is weaponized and the states have integrated the air into their structural violence. It means that the stifling political structures target not only the bodies of the migrants, Indigenous people, or political protestors, but also the whole environment they are in. The air has become a medium for terrorizing people.[11] The unequal right to breathe has led to a crisis in the reproduction of life:

> Under racial and extractive capitalism and imperialism, breathing has emerged as a medium that configures embodiment and experience as transductions of bio- and necropolitical forces—forces that optimize certain lives and trivialize or attack others.[12]

Sharpe and Simmons do not see anti-Black and anti-Indigenous racism as merely isolated processes but as integrated parts of the totality of the colonial atmospheric conditions. What Sharpe calls weather is the totality of the environments of combat breathing. It is an archive of breathlessness. The archive depicts the dispossession of air and stealing of breath as a main feature of slavery and its afterlife, of colonialism and the present coloniality of power. The archive historicizes breathlessness and demonstrates how breathing has become a white privilege. This is an archive from below or a counter-archive.

---

[10] Kristen Simmons, "Settler Atmospherics", Society for Cultural Anthropology, accessed 15 September 2022, https://culanth.org/fieldsights/settler-atmospherics.
[11] Peter Sloterdijk, "Airquakes", Environment and Planning D: *Society and Space* 27, no. 1 (1 February 2009): 41–57, https://doi.org/10.1068/dst1.
[12] Jean-Thomas Tremblay, *Breathing Aesthetics* (Durham: Duke University Press, 2022), 2.

Names of Death

In the official archive, a breathing body is faceless while a breathless one has a face. We did not know the name or the face of George Floyd before he was killed. We did not know about his combat breathing as a Black citizen in a racist society long before he was suffocated to death. We did not know the name or the face of Alan Kurdi, the three year old Syrian boy who drowned in the Mediterranean Sea when he was alive either, when he was undocumented and stateless. Black Americans, Indigenous people, travellers without papers and political prisoners are robbed of their faces while breathing and become visible to the rest of the world when breathless. Death gives bodies washed up on the shores of Europe, suffocated migrants in small shipping containers, or racialized bodies under the knees of white brutality a visibility they did not possess when alive. Death qualifies the unqualified. Death re-faces the de-faced.

Death demands stories and stories induce names and faces. Furthermore, the law commands documentation of the death. The law demands bodies. For its archive, the law demands a name and a face. The ancient Roman common law is *Habeas corpus,* which literally means "you shall have the body". The law demands the presence of the body. The politics of life is the politics of the body and the law demands to have the body.

But.... you are still breathing!

Sovereign power demands to possess your breath and thereby to control your words and claims. In Persian, the verb "daam zadan" means to breathe, and also to speak and to claim. A breath is a claim. Breathing is a struggle against racism, bordering practices, and political oppression. Not surprisingly, that breathing is perceived as subversive action.

You were never meant to breathe[13]

What would be strange is not whether the migrant drowns in the border sea, if the political dissident becomes silent, if the Black citizen is strangled to death by a white agent of law, but rather the contrary.

Tell us exactly why you still are breathing?

A British migration officer to an Ethiopian asylum seeker, "But they did not kill you."
A Swedish migration officer to an Afghan asylum seeker, "But the torture apparently was not very severe because you survived."
A Danish migration officer to an Iraqi woman, "You are alive now. You have not yet died."

You should die first and then you can claim your right to life. Being alive indicates a lack of credibility as far as one breathes, speaks, one claims. Breathing itself is enough to make one suspected. When David Dungay, the imprisoned Aboriginal Australian man, repeated "I can't breathe" before the air left his lungs, the officer replied, "If you can talk, you can breathe."

Tell us exactly why you can still talk?

The evidence for "I can't breathe" is death. If you cannot breathe and die then you are believed. Your claim of not being able to breathe is valid only when you do not breathe anymore.

---

[13] A paraphrase of "we were never meant to survive" by Audre Lorde in "A Litany for Survival", Audre Lorde, *The Black Unicorn:* Poems, Norton paperback (New York, NY: Norton, 1995).

Con-Spire

Colonization, as Fanon put it, is the occupation of daily pulsation, meaning that every single aspect of life becomes colonized and so 'living' per se becomes a political action.

Keeping breathing per se is an act of resistance against those who want to steal your breath. In such a condition of suffocation, breathing itself is part of the struggle for changing the weather of unbreathability. Combat breathing becomes a collective struggle to transform the occupied atmospheres and in so doing to cultivate more breathable worlds.[14]

Resistance generates new subjectivity. The struggle for liberation frees the colonized from the colonizer's violence but also from imaginations and self-images that have been imposed on her. As Fanon says, the resistance itself rather than the result is therapeutic and healing for traumatic experiences of racism and colonialism. Liberation can already be won during the struggle for it through breathing together.

A suffocating world generates resistance. "We can't breathe" has become a forceful political slogan by those who are the target of racist practices. The struggle for the right to breathe points to a fundamental political injustice. The conjunction of two political movements against anti-Black racism and anti-migrant racism, accentuates the collective struggles and engenders anti-colonial solidarity, for protecting lives and for the survival of the precarious groups.

Political and social movements that demand the right to breath today echo Fanon who, in the context of Vietnamese peasants' resistance against the US invasion, said that the colonized revolt because it has become impossible for them to breathe.[15] Protests by refugees in Australia's detention centre on Manus Island

---

[14] Jennifer Gabrys, "'Introduction: Atmospheric Citizens: How to Make Breathable Worlds'", in *Citizens of Worlds* (Minneapolis: University of Minnesota Press, Forthcoming).

[15] Frantz Fanon, *Black Skin, White Masks* (London: Pluto Press, 1986), 226.

in Papua New Guinea, and in Moria camp in Lesbos in Greece, through Kakuma refugee camp in Kenya, to the protests by poor farmers in Isfahan or to protests by Black and Indigenous groups in the USA, all trigger new frontiers for protecting life, demanding what Achille Mbembe calls, a "universal right to breath".[16]

The word conspiracy is combination of two Latin words, *con* and *spirare* meaning "to breathe together". Simmons sees conspiracy as a potential tactic to challenge the order of the things.[17] We should conspire against the toxic atmospherics we should conspire, breathe together and turn the air into a medium of solidarity and action. This is what Ranabir Samaddar calls "bio-politics from below",[18] i.e. a collective, solidarity-based response to the crisis of life, such as the current pandemic crisis, but also to the threat of colonial racism, political oppression, and fossil capitalism, all representing harms and the impending premature death.

The collective solidarity to care for living humans and non-humans demands access to air. Air is life itself. In many languages the word for air or breath and soul is same, such as *pneuma* in the ancient Greek. In a large part of the Middle East the word "nafas" or "nefes" (originated from Arabic) refers both to breath and spirit.

Caring for the air also means caring for the soul. In Persian the phrase "havaye kasi ra dashtan" (literally "to have someone's air") means to care and to protect someone. The word "hamdam" refers to the one you breathe with, a mate, a friend, a lover. In Xhosa (one of the official languages of South Africa and Zimbabwe) the word "phefumla" means soul and the verb "phefumlo" means not only breathing but also to mourn by speaking of the pains that weigh on someone.[19] Breath connects the material and the spiritual, the corporeal

---

[16] Achille Mbembe, "The Universal Right to Breathe", in *Critical Inquiry,* 47(2), 2021, 58–62.
[17] Simmons, "Settler Atmospherics".
[18] Ranabir Samaddar, *A Pandemic and the Politics of Life* (New Dehli: Women Unlimited, 2021), https://www.womenunlimited.net/Catalogue/academic_77.htm.
[19] Allen Feldman, "Memory Theaters, Virtual Witnessing, and the Trauma-Aesthetic", *Biography* 27, no. 1 (2004): 163–202.

and the emotional. Breath not only moulds the body through physical acts of inhalation and exhalation, but it also shapes immaterial relations to others (humans as well as non-humans) and to the self.

Omotayo T. Jolaosho's reflection on the "urgency of Black breath" depicts breathing as a practice of mobilization to "reclaim a world that has not been faithful to Black freedom by denying that most fundamental human need: breath".[20] As the feminist scholar and activist Sara Ahmed articulates, to breathe freely is an aspiration and "with breath comes imagination. With breath comes possibility. If queer politics is about freedom, it might simply mean the freedom to breathe".[21] Claiming the right to breathe freely is a subversive practice to liberate oneself from subjection.

Hope is in the air. Every single breath is impregnated with hope. In English, "aspiration" means both breath and hope. The hope to turn the toxic and hostile atmospherics into an atmosphere for solidarity practices and to mobilize and organize collective breathing.

Steal Back your Stolen Breath

This essay traces different but interrelated experiences of combat breathing, from Iran, through the Mediterranean Sea to the USA. Hostile atmospherics include all materialities and practices that have turned breathing into a combat, from Standing Rock to the Zayadneh-rud riverbed; from the asphyxiation of George Floyd and David Dungay to the suffocation of Pham Thi Tra My; from the unequal respiratory impacts of COVID-19 to the stealing of an Iranian poet's air.

It brings the individual and isolated experiences of combat breathing together to historicize them and to reveal the practice of dispossession of breath across

---

[20] Omotayo T. Jolaosho, "The Enduring Urgency of Black Breath", *Anthropology News* (blog), 16 April 2021, https://www.anthropology-news.org/articles/the-enduring-urgency-of-black-breath/.

[21] Sara Ahmed, *The Promise of Happiness* (Durham, NC: Duke University Press, 2010), 120, https://www.dukeupress.edu/The-Promise-of-Happiness/, 120.

space and time. Following the traces between fragmented experiences of breathlessness shows how they are connected to each other and thereby provides us with a constellation in which these fragments intersect. The constellation visualizes a diagnosis of the present. Respiratory inequalities and asphyxiation are designed by a racial neoliberalism, causing an atmospheric differentiation between those with surplus breathing right and those for whom breathing has become a struggle.[22] Combat breathing is a practice that connects struggles across bodies, histories, and environments.[23]

The archive of stolen breaths is an attempt to visualize these traces and the pattern of dispossession of air from people in different contexts. By juxtaposing different cases of breathlessness, the archive of stolen breaths demonstrates a set of relations. Following Ariella Azoulay, I use the archive not as a collection of isolated fragments from a completed past but rather as a space of shared life where the past is always incomplete and the present always in becoming.[24] It is an archive of shared life because the air is always shared. Air and breath have been stolen from people under political and colonial oppression. Stolen breaths are an analytical and political tool that links different experiences across time and space. The verb "stolen" provides us a tool to approach the subject of breathlessness in relation to colonial practices, fossil capitalism and racism. Using the term stolen and emphasising how people's breath is stolen, denaturalizes what is otherwise naturalized, and politicizes what is otherwise depoliticized. The archive of stolen breaths reminds us that to breathe means to speak, to claim and to practice hope.

---

[22] Chloé Ahmann and Alison Kenner, "Breathing Late Industrialism", in: *Engaging Science, Technology, and Society,* 6, 2020, 416–438.
[23] Gabrys, *Citizens of Worlds.*
[24] Azoulay, Ariella, "Archive", in *Political Concepts, a Critical Lexicon,* The New School, 1, no. Winter (2011).

References

Ahmed, Sara. *The Promise of Happiness*. Durham, NC: Duke University Press, 2010. https://www.dukeupress.edu/The-Promise-of-Happiness/.

Apata, Gabriel O. "'I Can't Breathe': The Suffocating Nature of Racism". *Theory, Culture & Society* 37, no. 7–8 (1 December 2020): 241–54. https://doi.org/10.1177/0263276420957718.

Azoulay, Ariella. "Archive". *Political Concepts, a Critical Lexicon,* The New School, 1, no. Winter (2011).

Baker, Mike, Jennifer Valentino-DeVries, Manny Fernandez, and Michael LaForgia. "Three Words. 70 Cases. The Tragic History of 'I Can't Breathe.'" *The New York Times,* 29 June 2020, sec. U.S. https://www.nytimes.com/interactive/2020/06/28/us/i-cant-breathe-police-arrest.html.

Borja, Andrea Garcia, Mohammedali Abunajela, Safa Msehli, and Jorge Galindo. "Deaths on Maritime Migration Routes to Europe Soar in First Half of 2021: IOM Brief". International Organization for Migration, 14 July 2021. https://www.iom.int/news/deaths-maritime-migration-routes-europe-soar-first-half-2021-iom-brief.

Crawley, Ashton T. *Blackpentecostal Breath*. New York: Fordham University Press, 2017.

Fanon, Frantz. *A Dying Colonialism*. Translated by Haakon Chevalier. Grove Press, 1967.

——— *Black Skin, White Masks*. London: Pluto Press, 1986.

Feldman, Allen. "Memory Theaters, Virtual Witnessing, and the Trauma-Aesthetic". *Biography* 27, no. 1 (2004): 163–202.

Gabrys, Jennifer. "Introduction: Atmospheric Citizens: How to Make Breathable Worlds". In *Citizens of Worlds*. Minneapolis: University of Minnesota Press, Forthcoming. https://manifold.umn.edu/read/introduction/section/ed78c911-1c1c-4f57-a296-520f5af50a38.

Jolaosho, Omotayo T. "The Enduring Urgency of Black Breath". *Anthropology News* (blog), 16 April 2021. https://www.anthropology-news.org/articles/the-enduring-urgency-of-black-breath/.

Lorde, Audre. *The Black Unicorn: Poems.* Norton paperback. New York, NY: Norton, 1995.

Mbembe, Achille. "The Universal Right to Breathe". *Critical Inquiry* 47(2) (2021): 58-62.

Rancière, Jacques. *Disagreement: Politics and Philosophy*. Translated by Julie Rose. Minneapolis: University of Minnesota Press, 1999.

Samaddar, Ranabir. *A Pandemic and the Politics of Life*. New Dehli: Women Unlimited, 2021. https://www.womenunlimited.net/Catalogue/academic_77.htm.

Sharpe, Christina. *In the Wake: On Blackness and Being*. Durham, NC: Duke University Press, 2016. https://doi.org/10.1215/9780822373452.

Simmons, Kristen. "Settler Atmospherics". Society for Cultural Anthropology. Accessed 15 September 2022. https://culanth.org/fieldsights/settler-atmospherics.

Sloterdijk, Peter. "Airquakes". Environment and Planning D: *Society and Space* 27, no. 1 (1 February 2009): 41–57. https://doi.org/10.1068/dst1.

Tremblay, Jean-Thomas. *Breathing Aesthetics*. Durham: Duke University Press, 2022.

Yildirim, Umut. "Breathing under Blockade: Displaced and Diasporic Ecologies in a Middle Eastern Heritage Site". *Current Anthropology,* Forthcoming.

Hope Ginsburg
Meditations on Amphibiousness

Fig. 1

Hope   Ginsburg

**Inhale, allowing wide-open awareness,
nothing to do, chest rising.
Exhale, bringing awareness to the breath,
grounding more deeply, chest falling.**

The connection between scuba diving and breath is a given. What about that of meditation and healing to diving—and on land for that matter? From 2014 to 2020, I produced a series of fifteen *Land Dives* exploring the practice of mindfulness—defined here as awareness of one's present-moment experience without judgment—as a way of attuning to the catastrophe of climate change. What follows is the backstory of how I came to make this work and, borrowing from scuba parlance, a "log" of the project's key dives.

I learned to scuba dive so that I could see sponges. From 2006 to 2016, I worked on a pedagogical project called *Sponge,* which took that porous sea creature as a muse for knowledge exchange. Sponges are filter-feeders, breaking down tiny particles from the ocean's water even further and expelling them as nourishment for other reef creatures. They are great "exchangers". They are also the first multicellular organism; it's not a leap to propose the sponge as an originating model of collectivity. The *Sponge* project reflected its namesake by comprising numerous collaborative endeavors and focusing on knowledge exchange through workshops, events, and classes. I became so enamored with sponges that I wanted to witness them alive on the reef.

My 2011 dive training occurred at the end of recovery from a fractured sternum and vertebra in a car accident. The ability to walk with the heavy tank on my back and swim with it torquing my spine signaled healing. A conceptual link between diving and healing was forged. A year and a half later, a dive off the coast of Guanica, Puerto Rico added meditation to that constellation. During a shallow dive on a bed of soft corals, my breath was timed exactly to the sway of the animals in the surge. I inhaled; the sea fans and feathery sea whips swayed to the left. I exhaled; they bent back to the right. I became aware of my breath as never before. Breathing with the ocean in that way was an unforgettable meditation.

Arriving the following summer at a Rauschenberg Residency on Captiva, Florida, I was keen for a shift in my work after focusing on the *Sponge* project for eight years. I imagined a more personal turn, making an underwater video reenactment of the accident that led to my injuries. Slow-moving divers' bodies would stand in for multiple cars on a fast highway. As I planned potential shots for that video, I had an image in my mind of a group of people meditating on land with scuba gear. My fellow residents were game to try it, and I set about orienting them to rented scuba gear and giving them simple meditation instructions. What followed was a workshop remarkably akin to *Sponge* activities, and a group meditation with scuba gear that was unexpectedly effective. We practiced mindfulness of the breath, a common anchor used to focus attention in meditation. The scuba gear heightened breath-awareness, delivering each inhalation with an audible rush of air. It was difficult to lose connection to the breath with the scuba apparatus calling attention to it. And the mild to moderate discomfort of the equipment—its weight, warmth, and physical constraints—kept us grounded in our bodies. The shared impact of this "mediated" meditation made an impression on each of us and pointed to a new direction for the project. The original concept for the video dissolved, and the project that was to become "Land Dive Team" emerged.

For *Breathing on Land: Zekreet, Qatar,* a series of photographic stills made early in the spring of 2015 during an experimental early Land Dive, I meditated alone, breathing with scuba gear in an expansive desert landscape. As disjunctive as the images appear, they contain the ominous implication of a "future ocean" as rising sea levels threaten the Persian Gulf region. From a first-person point of view, that meditation experience included a moment of startling silence. As the sounds of SUVs and all of the other people there that day disappeared in the wind—the attraction was a monolithic series of Richard Serra sculptures—I had the feeling of total aloneness. Drawing breath from a tank on my back, I resisted the urge to look up, practiced concentration through mindfulness of breath, and gazed at the patch of rocky sand before me.

Land Dive Team: Rice Rivers Center Wetlands, also 2015, presents a small group meditation at the Virginia Commonwealth University (VCU) Rice Rivers Center, a biological field station outside Richmond, Virginia. This meditation was the pilot "deployment" of the "Land Dive Team," which would publicly gather in sites lending themselves to environmental interpretation. Three of us meditated in muddy wetlands, the site of a massive initiative to restore a landscape decimated by nineteen-twenties damming. Seventy acres of tidal and non-tidal freshwater wetlands had been flooded, destroying critical habitats of the lower James River ecosystem, including the bald cypress and tupelo gum of the swamp forest. In this remediated terrain, we were acutely aware of the changing light, birds circling overhead, and the slowly rising tide. We also learned that the mud caking our wetsuits had a scandalous history, one of the first of its kind to play out nationally. Hopewell, Virginia,

Fig. 2

just upriver from the Rice, was the site of a chemical company, producing between three and six thousand pounds of insecticide a day in the nineteen-seventies, dumping waste directly into the river. This led to a chemical and medical crisis and the onset of commercial fishing bans in the area. With bans now lifted, along with the Kimages Creek dam, the site is in recovery. *Rice Rivers Center Wetlands* is the first edited Land Dive Team video with sound and began an enduring collaboration with the director of photography Matt Flowers and composer and sound recordist Joshua Quarles.

The slow rise of the tidal James River during our wetlands meditation led to the idea for *Land Dive Team: Bay of Fundy,* 2016. The piece is a single-channel video with sound that focuses on four people (including myself) in seated meditation, breathing through scuba gear at the shore of the Bay of Fundy. The bay is known for having the highest tidal rise on the planet, rising and falling up to fifty feet a day at the head of the bay in the Minas Basin. In this Land Dive, filmed at the coast of New Brunswick, Canada, divers sit in a row, their gaze focused in front of them. As the cold tide flows in, they are rocked by the waves and hear the chorus of breath drawn through scuba regulators. The water rises on their bodies until they completely disappear below, leaving only their breaths hitting the surface of the water. These clusters of bubbles are documented in *Breath Portraits I–VII,* a separate photographic series. After we shot the video in October of 2015, the Conservation Council of New Brunswick reported that day as having the highest King Tide ever recorded in the Gulf

Fig. 3

of Maine. Such shifts in the tides and changes in the temperature of the Bay of Fundy further evoke the anxiety of catastrophic climate change that underpins the video. There is an individual psychological dimension to the piece as well, as the divers sit steadfast, drawing breath after breath from the finite tank of air, even as the water continues to rise.

Land Dive Team: Amphibious James, 2018, extended the focus of the project to other species. Commissioned by the Institute for Contemporary Art at VCU and the Richmond Symphony, *Amphibious James* was a meditation with the river and the beings in its waters, on its shores, and in the air above. The live, site-specific performance comprised three groups of performers and took place in three parts. A wind ensemble played collaborator Joshua Quarles's score, a Land Dive Team meditated on the shore with scuba gear, and an Amphibious Dive Team with amplified telecommunications gear transmitted a spoken meditation from within the river. During the first act, the audience heard the sounds of the Land Divers' breaths, the wind ensemble, and pre-recorded field sounds from alongside the James River as the Amphibious Dive Team made its way to the river. Act two included the submerged guided meditation, an invitation for viewers to bring attention to their breath, joining the musicians, divers, and all nearby creatures—breathing through gills, skin, and lungs. The words mixed with the score and field recordings taken from water-dwelling species. The meditation script concluded by thanking viewers for "cultivating [their] amphibiousness, [their] awareness of

Fig. 4

this air, this land, this water." The work ended when the divers surfaced and made their way back to the Land Dive Team onshore, amidst the elegiac third movement and a chorus of pre-recorded frogs. Human breath moved fluidly from land to water and back again. The piece asks what it means to "breathe with" the creatures with whom we share our environment, proposing amphibiousness—mediated and actual—as an analog for multispecies awareness.

The sponge as muse returned with *Land Dive Team: Tarpon Springs,* 2020, the second to last work in the series and a collaboration with Joshua Quarles. The piece was sited at the historic Sponge Exchange of Tarpon Springs, Florida, the epicenter of the late nineteenth and early twentieth-century sponge industry in the United States. The opportunity to make a Land Dive at this site—its name an uncanny reference to the knowledge exchange of the *Sponge* project and its location adjacent to some of the most plentiful sponge beds on the planet—was a thrill. Though I first visited Tarpon Springs as a child, I made a research trip during my Rauschenberg Residency in 2014, at the height of *Sponge* and the outset of *Land Dive Team*. *Land Dive Team: Tarpon Springs* afforded the opportunity to think through the relationship between the two bodies of work, as well as between sponge biology and meditation. The site-specific performance drew a connection between the movement of breath and sound through the meditating bodies of participants and the flow of ocean water through the pores of a sea sponge. Composer

Joshua Quarles wrote and performed a new wind instrument score for clarinet and saxophone in three movements. An excerpt transcribed from the performative meditation introduction offered to viewers follows:
Sponges have no inside or outside! They are all pores: the phylum Porifera. Their entire bodies are penetrable by the water around them. Good, bad, terrifying, ecstatic, everything passes through them—arises and flows through—they are a glorious model of non-attachment—if you will, the ultimate meditators—ever-present to all unfolding in their world—and they do not move—totally still, in perpetual experience of their surroundings. Think of what we can learn from this kindred species. Your breath

Fig. 5

moving through you, sounds moving through you, are as water moving through the pores of a sponge. Can you return to that thought as your mind wanders—which of course, it will.

Land Dive Team: Tarpon Springs took place in late February of 2020, just before the COVID-19 pandemic took hold in the United States. The fifteenth and final iteration in the Land Dive Team body of work took place at Smith College in Northampton, Massachusetts on March 10, 2020. Participants in full scuba gear intercepted an email from the college announcing the campus shutdown due to the virus just before making their way to a populous campus atrium to meditate with tanks of their own air to breathe.

Learning through *Land Dive Team* fueled insight into the relationship between meditation and our climate in crisis. Over the six-year course of the project, my own meditation practice developed, I dove deeper into the

Fig. 6

Buddhist teachings that guide the work, and trained to lead mindfulness sessions for others. In concluding the narrative arc of the project, I'd like to offer a few connections between the somatic, spiritual and ecological, which signal current projects and further investigation. Mindfulness is a practice of paying attention and attuning with acceptance to what is arising in the present moment. This is a somatic awareness, including that which may be extremely difficult to sit with in the felt sense of the body. A cultivated capacity to stay with difficulty in one's own system has a direct bearing on the ability to meet struggle in others and in the world. An ability to discern skillful modes of engagement emerges. In the Buddhist view of interdependence, the very notion of self and other is nondual. Ecology offers another apt context for exploring this interdependence. Finally, our own nervous systems are understood to impact the collective nervous system. Through practice, a sense of individualism erodes and connection to other living beings and systems—as well as compassion for their suffering—arises. In meditation, there is training in staying with what we might otherwise push away, discerning skillful approaches, and discovering and regulating our non-separateness. Proposed is that these fruits of practice can be equipment for turning toward the collective and unequally distributed crisis of a radically changing climate.

Fig. 1 — Hope Ginsburg
Breathing on Land: Beach I, 2014
Documentation from the first Land Dive
Support provided by the Rauschenberg Residency/Robert Rauschenberg Foundation

Fig. 2 — Hope Ginsburg
Breathing on Land: Zekreet, Qatar III, 2015
Archival ink jet print
19 × 26 in.

Fig. 3 — Hope Ginsburg
Land Dive Team: Rice Rivers Center Wetlands, 2015
Still from single-channel video with sound
5 min. 5 sec.

Fig. 4 — Hope Ginsburg
Land Dive Team: Bay of Fundy, 2016
Still from single-channel video projection with sound
7 min. 8 sec.
Support provided by the Film/Video Studio Program at the Wexner Center for the Arts

Fig. 5 — Hope Ginsburg with Composer Joshua Quarles
Land Dive Team: Amphibious James, 2018
Still from site-specific, public performance
Approx. 22 min.
Image credit: UFOClub Creative

Fig. 6 — Hope Ginsburg and Joshua Quarles
Land Dive Team: Tarpon Springs, 2020
Still from site-specific, public performance
Approx. 20 min.
Image credit: Pat Blocher

Emily Beausoleil

Breathing Space —Germinations of Decolonial Allyship

"When you are not supposed to live, as you are, where you are, with whom you are with, then survival is a radical action." — Sara Ahmed

"Another world is not only possible, she is on her way. On a quiet day I can hear her breathing." — Arundhati Roy

Introduction

I live and breathe in a body that, in order of sensed experience, is middle-aged, able, white, female. My tongue easily wraps around Anglo acoustics, via a Canadian accent; my blue eyes and blonde hair connect me to peoples from far distant lands that presumed to claim the whole world as home. I have lived now in Aotearoa New Zealand for nearly a decade—which, when it takes seven years for a body to forge itself anew, means my body is now made of the materiality of this place. Yet I do not claim to be of this place; for

> there is no body as such that is given in the world: bodies materialise in a complex set of temporal and spatial relations to other bodies, including bodies that are recognised as familiar, familial and friendly, and those that are considered strange.[1]

My bodily experience, in this place and with this familial history, is shaped both by long histories and habits of obliviousness to the historical and structural conditions that differently shape our lives—what Mark Rifkin calls 'settler common sense'[2]—and a more recent history of learning to attend to what has long gone unsensed. I use this body in this recent phase of life to actively work against, unpick and rework, settler-colonial blindnesses and entitlements that are still carried at the level of cellular memory, muscular propensities, and broader structural channels that make such obliviousness the path of least resistance, and not only socially acceptable, but rewarded.[3]

---

[1] Sara Ahmed, *Strange Encounters: Embodied Others in Post-Coloniality* (London: Routledge, 2000), 40.
[2] Mark Rifkin, *Settler Common Sense: Queerness and Everyday Colonialism in the American Renaissance,* 1st edition (Minneapolis; London: University of Minnesota Press, 2014).
[3] José Medina, *The Epistemology of Resistance: Gender and Racial Oppression, Epistemic Injustice, and Resistant Imaginations,* 1st edition (Oxford: Oxford University Press, 2012).

It is from this body that I write, on this cold and bright winter's day in the southern hemisphere in 2021. I write with and about the limitations of enacting decolonial and decolonising allyship by bodies such as this, and share early intimations for me of what, perhaps, such allyship can look like. To do this, I offer an account of different 'economies of breath' within settler-colonialism that can mean that those who breathe easily within an unjust world can cause further harm within gestures of solidarity. Drawing on my own recent experience of profound misstep within such a gesture, I then offer three ways this mistake reoriented my sense of what effective solidarity requires, insights that could only—for a body like this—be learned through experience. In the spirit of this volume, I would like to articulate these as three ways that settlers seeking to contribute to a decolonial future might understand this work as 'letting it breathe': firstly, a lesson on the crucial importance of learning to cede control and shift the centre of gravity, contributing to decentring whiteness and settler dominance by giving space for and being led by what and who you are not; second, a lesson regarding the recalibration away from western markers of outcome and impact to prioritise instead what is truly most essential—survival of and care for living relational bodies; and finally, a lesson regarding the need to remain in the face of challenge, to continue to work despite the mistakes—for the lessons bodies like mine must learn are lifelong, indeed intergenerational.

Economies of Breath

> "Part of what it means to be indigenous in this world is that your heart breaks all the time. This is why acknowledging our positionality is so important, because it tells us where you are in relation to the heartbreak." — Emalani Case

Walking back from our neighbourhood mosque on March 16th 2019, where we laid flowers and words of support before an empty house of worship and stood with the crowd in silent solidarity with those who had been targets of terrorism in Christchurch the day before, I remember strategizing about ways to engage the broader community to address racism and Islamophobia. I did not realise that even the presumption of safety to walk these streets and congregate in a mourning crowd testified to the wholly particular phenomenology of being in a white body. And the speed with which I ricocheted off heartbreak into agentic planning, planning that entailed gathering in public, was further evidence that in this body, I experience a default safety and sense of entitlement to physical space and political agency. This immediate trauma was not felt, by me, to the same degree as those in Muslim bodies; it did not layer and compound with previous traumas from my own life or across generations, to refract and intensify and debilitate. Put differently, and inspired by poet and scholar-activist Emalani Case's words during a lecture she gave this year on settler-colonialism on her home island of Hawai'i, my urgency to act and presumption of the capacity to do so was borne of my specific "relation to the heartbreak".

In *Strange Encounters,* Sara Ahmed describes the "economies of touch"[4] that structure our embodied relationalities and, in turn, relations within the social body. Profoundly structured inequalities that are sustained or, in rarer moments, challenged via embodied sense experience, regarding who feels familiar or strange, who we hold close or at bay, whose differences we seek to expel or vilify and whose we let affect us. For this chapter, I would like to offer the notion of "economies of breath" to draw attention to and facilitate reflexivity regarding how these self-same historical, structural inequalities also produce differential capacities to breathe. For those whose bodies are unmarked, who experience themselves as "bodies-at-home or bodies-in-place",[5] breathing comes easily. In fact, it is almost altogether unnoticed, this ease. Here, I am thinking of differential economies of breath in two senses: both one's literal breath as it fills the lungs, the ease of which signals a sympathetic or parasympathetic state in the autonomic nervous system, by which a body communicates with itself that everything is or is not right and safe in the world; but also of the uneven distribution of being able to take basic survival and its conditions for granted—the absence or presence of forms of 'slow violence'[6] that make bare life difficult and uncertain. To be able to experience oneself as a body-at-home is also to breathe easily both in situ and in the broader sense of having the luxury of inattention regarding the core conditions of sustaining one's life.

This is, perhaps, an inversion of Judith Butler's theorizations of precarity. As Butler articulates so well, while all bodies are always on some level and at some moments—sickness, injury, loss, death—especially precarious, precarity is also unevenly distributed throughout the social body.[7] Engaging with Butler's work, Janell Watson puts it this way:

> Corporeal fragility both equalises and differentiates: all bodies are menaced by suffering, injury, and death (precariousness), but some bodies are more protected and others more exposed (precarity). Precariousness is shared by all; precarity is 'distributed unequally'.[8]

[4] Ahmed, *Strange Encounters,* 49.
[5] Ahmed, 46.
[6] Rob Nixon, *Slow Violence and the Environmentalism of the Poor* (Cambridge, Mass: Harvard University Press, 2011). Caitlin Cahill and Rachel Pain, "Representing Slow Violence and Resistance: On Hiding and Seeing", *ACME: An International Journal for Critical Geographies* 18, no. 5 (3 October 2019): 1054–65.
[7] Judith Butler, *Frames of War: When Is Life Grievable?* (London: Verso, 2009), 25.
[8] Butler, 1.

Our shared experience of vulnerability, then, is not evenly shared. In Emalani Case's terms, we are all differently positioned in relation to heartbreak.[9] Drawing attention to the capacity to breathe easily focuses attention on relative advantages and resources that are tacitly within this account of precarity, vulnerability, and heartbreak. Like the study of historical privilege rather than simply historical trauma, an economy of breath can sensitize advantaged groups to what often and easily slips from view precisely because of the ways that social advantage operates. Advantage, manifest in the ability to breathe easily both in the immediacy of the physical body and in maintaining the ongoing conditions of one's life, is by nature unsensed by those who have it. Kimmell,[10] Moewaka Barnes et al.,[11] and others characterise historical privilege—the "inherited cushions and footholds"[12] that engender opportunities and protect against incidental losses—as a "breeze at my back." And while headwinds are all too apparent to anyone struggling to navigate them, tailwinds that move with us along the pathways of our various projects are almost altogether insensible. Breathing easily, whether in the moment or as one navigates the world, by nature goes unnoticed. Attending to this inattention, then, helps draw into view the very capacity for oversight of dimensions of sociopolitical life, as it is experienced at the level of everyday embodied experience. And this language of different capacities to breathe more or less easily helps alert us—me—to how this presumption of breath can lead to lightning-quick oversight of and thus pressures upon the struggles for breath others may be experiencing, positioned differently as they are within the same socio-structural conditions.

Faltering Allyship

What does this mean for allyship? First and foremost, for me it has meant profound missteps. To move through the world as one who breathes easily and yet fails to sense either this ease or that it is not widely shared can mean that how we—I—respond to witnessed injustice and struggle can cause further trauma, strain, and shortness of breath.
One recent experience illustrates this most clearly. In response to observing a conference to explore the possibility of a climate citizens' assembly here in Aotearoa,

---

[9] Emalani Case, *Everything Ancient Was Once New: Indigenous Persistence from Hawai'i to Kahiki, Everything Ancient Was Once New* (University of Hawaii Press, 2021).
[10] Michael S. Kimmel, "Toward a Sociology of the Superordinate: This Breeze at My Back", in *Privilege: A Reader*, 4th Edition (New York: Routledge, 2018), 1–13.
[11] Helen Moewaka Barnes, Belinda Borell, and Time McCreanor, "Theorising the Structural Dynamics of Ethnic Privilege in Aotearoa: Unpacking 'This Breeze at My Back' (Kimmell and Ferber 2003)", *International Journal of Critical Indigenous Studies* 7, no. 1 (1 January 2014): 1–14.
[12] Christine Sleeter, "Inheriting Footholds and Cushions: Family Legacies and Institutional Racism", *Counterpoints* 449 (2014): 11–26.

journalist and poet Nadine Anne Hura (Ngāti Hine, Ngāpuhi) raised concerns regarding the potential of the proposed designs for a climate assembly being neo-colonial. She observed that plans to mount such an enterprise here showed all signs of reproducing colonising dynamics: from the use of random selection and demographic 'representativeness' in a country where the "indigenous population has already been decimated by colonisation," to the question of who counts as an 'expert' consulted within the process; to unaddressed challenges of access, trust, and even contending ontologies for Māori communities; to the presumption that robust forms of deliberation do not already exist in this place, and that Māori would be invited into a pre-crafted western process. But drawing attention to these risks and propensities was not an intellectual exercise, for Hura. These critiques emerged because the designs proposed, and the quick-moving, presentist energy of those proposing them, offered no place for her father or her brother, and the lives they lead; they neglected and, when challenged, glazed over the inability of such designs to account for and be accountable to these lives and the broader context of Māori sovereignty and colonisation, with climate change presenting merely the most recent chapter of the latter.[13]

As a deliberative scholar, and one seeking to increasingly orient my work to the Māori context in which I do it, I was so struck by the importance of these critiques, and the need for people like me to hear them. So when my colleague Max Rashbrooke—someone who is a strong advocate for participatory democracy here in Aotearoa New Zealand—mentioned he was planning to write a public response to Hura's critiques, I suggested we write something together. While Rashbrooke was interested in clarifying the methods of deliberation to alleviate concerns about its benefits and risks, I wished to write on behalf of and for western deliberative folk by enacting a listening and response, a reception and step forward, to meet the challenges of the piece. We merged these voices into one, which included Rashbrooke's sketches of possible deliberative adaptations in light of Hura's critiques, as well as my caveats that the two of us

> cannot sketch out exactly how all that would work—nor would we seek to. But whatever happens, we cannot simply adopt the idea of a citizens' assembly wholesale: we have to ask what it means *to do this right, here*.[14]

Before it was printed, I sent Hura the article, expressing my appreciation for what she had written and my hopes that the forthcoming response made this clear and demonstrated that people like me were listening.

---

[13] Nadine Anne Hura, "Who Gets to Be an 'Ordinary New Zealander'? On Citizens' Assemblies, Climate Change and Tangata Whenua", The Spinoff, 23 November 2019, https://thespinoff.co.nz/atea/23-11-2019/who-gets-to-be-an-ordinary-new-zealander-on-citizens-assemblies-climate-change-and-tangata-whenua.
[14] The article from which this quotation is taken is no longer publicly available.

I had been so sure that the article would be read this way. That confidence tells me now about how little I still understand and how far I have to go. The article evoked the very opposite response from key Māori public commentators on Twitter, who read it as "whitesplaining" and "academic objectification" of Hura by those with "no skin in the game".[15] As Tina Ngata wrote,

> You [Hura] had come into that space as a wahine Maori seeking to understand in a noa way, with all of the hesitancy and scepticism that we all carry in our bones from 250 years of maltreatment. Our concerns are not objective, nor academic, nor theoretical.... And your writing reflected that. Our concerns are visceral, and current. We are facing violence, death, incarceration, child loss, land loss, EVERY DAY and that's what we shoulder when we walk into these spaces that are so rarely provided with US in mind.[16]

With gratitude to these vocal critics who said "things I couldn't seem to find my voice to articulate," Hura affirmed that this is also how she had experienced the article—condescending rather than acknowledging, silencing rather than amplifying, and a failure to "engag[e] with the humanity of my father and my bro".[17]

I share this spectacular failure in the hopes that it can teach more than just myself about how efforts to respond to, support, and amplify Indigenous voices can in fact do the very opposite. In this case, what is clearer to me now than it was then comes back to this sense of unequal economies of breath: what was interesting to me, what was an intellectual exercise regarding abstract models and hypothetical future endeavours, was a matter of life and death, and the merest edge of vast and ongoing struggle for others. What piqued curiosity and kindled a 'turning towards' within one body, this body, touched on the longest of histories and deepest of wounds to another. And what I moved quickly on—merely glancing at later edits by my co-author because I gave academic writing

---

[15] Tina Ngata, "Wow. @TheSpinoffTV Branching into Full-Blown Whitesplaining Now", Tweet, *Twitter,* 27 February 2020, https://twitter.com/tinangata/status/1232870126711558145. Kera Sherwood-O'Regan, "Yeah Super Cringey... like Umm on What Authority Are You Speaking on Matike Mai & Why Do a Response All This Time Later When You Haven't Actually Been Engaging with Our Communities on What Kōrero Have Been Happening since Nadine's Piece AND When You Have No Skin in the Game?", Tweet, *Twitter,* 27 February 2020, https://twitter.com/keraoregan/status/1232888520999493632. Tina Ngata, "All the Quals in the World Don't Matter", Tweet, *Twitter,* 28 February 2020, https://twitter.com/tinangata/status/1232870126711558145.

[16] Ngata, "All the Quals in the World Don't Matter".

[17] Nadine Anne Hura, "Please Bear with Me as 5,000 Words Is More My Comfort Zone so Twitter Is a Challenge but I Really Wanted to Add Some Whakaaro to This Discussion about the Spinoff Piece Written" by @MaxRashbrooke and @BeausoleilEmily on CAs.', Tweet, *Twitter,* 27 February 2020, https://twitter.com/nadineannehura/status/1233141388071489538. Nadine Anne Hura, "Totally! Oh... Not at All I Was Actually Just Reacting to the Whole Wide Kōrero and My Disappointment That the Authors Never Engaged with the Humanity of My Father and My Bro, Which Your Thread Highlighted for Me, but i'm New to Twitter so Sometimes Retweet the Wrong Thing Lol", Tweet, *Twitter,* 27 February 2020, https://twitter.com/nadineannehura/status/1233135200256684032.

priority—was engaging the most precious of loved ones and most serious of realities.

I sought a meeting of minds as sign of respect; in doing so, I disrespected so much that gesture cast aside, of the all-too-personal and whole-of-structure and history, of the highest of stakes. And in co-writing with another Pākehā (European NZ settler) deliberative 'expert,' I mobilised both academic power and whiteness; this was not a harmless meeting of minds, it was a public counter to one of the few wāhine Māori (Māori women) journalists, who had in fact offered stories of her most beloved ones to present important challenges to a dominant group about the most current of colonising movements. We do not meet on equal ground, or simply as individuals—indeed, as western liberals often presume, as mere disembodied minds—in the context of the present moment; and it is because of the easy breath of this body, this physical and structural body I inhabit that I could even mistake this to be so. We do not meet with the same relation to the heartbreak, my breath so easy I could mistake as intellectual or abstracted exercise what is "visceral, and current," what pulses with ongoing and as-yet unmet pain. As Hura shared with me later,

> The hurt that our people feel when words inadvertently cause harm is real, but it's the culmination of hurt; it's 200 years of hurt. It's like a bruise; the original wound may not have been caused by those who came after, but sometimes even the barest touch can cause pain.
> (1 March 2020, personal communication)[18]

Even as these public critiques and direct mail I received over these days made my pulse race, my breath short, my whole body flush hot, even as it caused a precise sensation of precarity, exposing my ability to live and work in this place as highly contingent and fragile, I realise now that this sense of insecurity and shortness of breath were still momentary: the exception to the rule. And because of settler dominance in this country, I realised that should I refocus my attention in other directions as an academic, I could potentially avoid such sensations altogether. Now, months later, being with those sensations and implications remains something I can 'opt in' to—and out of. Nothing in my lived experience can come close to the heartbreak of which Case speaks, the heartbreak of and from which Hura wrote. My wading into this terrain with obliviousness to this meant that my effort to meet and amplify another in fact caused further harm and silencing. How might an attunement to the radically unequal economies of breath among those who, like me, breathe easily change how we come to such encounters? How can attending to and being guided by our radically different relations to the

---

[18] Nadine Anne Hura has given me permission to share this from our email correspondence.

heartbreak help people like me come to more rightful relationship and accountability to those for who live most closely to it?

But there is one further way focusing on the 'breath' may teach something here. Hura noted in her public response on Twitter that she wondered "why in all of this [Emily] didn't just email me and say, 'hey, wanna grab lunch?' Because whakawhanaungatanga [relationship-building] doesn't happen over email and it's not as complicated as it sounds".[19] I had sought to build a bridge and further a public conversation in the most formal and public of forums—national media. And when I sent her the article privately, I had not even thought to propose meeting in person, or even to offer the piece as an open question, as something (and someone) Hura might be interested in engaging in a more dialogic and indeed personal way. I was so surprised by this comment by Hura, and surprised by my surprise. I wrote her privately after this, to ask if, in fact, it was still possible to go for that lunch together. Hura responded with such profound generosity that it felt like we truly met, through the correspondence that has followed between us over the years since. I count myself very fortunate to have connected with her, as two particular people, who also carry with us histories and structures that are always-already in our bodies, in the room, and, indeed, in how we come to meet. I had discounted the importance of the particular meeting and personal relationship, just as I had been oblivious to high, constant, and personal stakes in relation to the heartbreak. Simply to meet together, us two—over a meal, in the quiet corner of a day rather than the glare of public discourse. To focus on the relationship, the real and living relationship between two people, rather than the play of ideas. This is something I am learning about, too, as a settler here in Aotearoa New Zealand: relationships first and foremost, the breathing in and out of personal relationships as the very way we orient, remain accountable, and learn to stand upright in an unjust world.

Letting it Breathe

Hā ki roto, hā ki waho
Breathe in, breathe out

In light of this experience, three directions for a more attuned solidarity feel, to me, to be potentially generative. All of these might be characterised as, in different ways, learning to 'let it breathe.' Firstly, solidarity by bodies like mine, that breathe easily and thus stand at great distance from heartbreak, should likely curb any instinct to rush to act in public in the early stages of activism, unless alongside and led by Indigenous communities. This is not to say don't act, and there are many forms of active response besides very public individual actions

---

[19] Hura, "Totally!".

like the one I chose to take. But particularly for those accustomed or incentivized to having a public voice, as academics are, I believe there is a lesson here in learning to move more slowly, and more behind the scenes in demonstrations of support, particularly early on. Most simply, this is because bodies like mine are still learning, have so much to learn, and often what needs to be learned is precisely that which is misrepresented in settler societies as simpler or less significant than what it is. This means that what can feel like realization can, in fact, only be the very first layer of something that runs much, much deeper. Moreover, it can require radical reorientation from long-habituated tendencies to presume the context in which such encounters and learning occur are one's own, and thus understood. In this misplaced effort to acknowledge and respond to challenge, my co-author and I invoked what was and remains unknown and perhaps always unknowable to us, both in terms of the heartbreak and the Māori ontology and authority that were calling our ways of working into account. And we reasserted settler dominance in our mode of listening to these challenges, because we held these in ways that minimised the enormity of what they are.

This experience called me up short. It exposed how very little I understand about the things of which I spoke. And it revealed to me the importance of *not* working in public: the need for much more time dedicated to listening, learning, and being reworked in light of that learning; the need to work on relationships, out of the glare of public platforms. I am immensely grateful for this challenge—it precipitated a refreshed humility and reorientation about where I am. It led me to go deeper, over these years, in my learning about Matike Mai Aotearoa,[20] the Māori-led vision for constitutional transformation of which Hura wrote in her article and of which we presumed to speak in turn. It has led to participating in and eventually co-facilitating communities of learning and accountability for other Pākehā seeking to understand and support that vision. And this has, in turn, changed what and how I teach as a Politics lecturer with my students, why I now often decline or recommend others for public speaking engagements, and only speak publicly regarding this terrain either where expressly invited by Māori or where I focus on 'claiming our bad kin'[21] and furthering the work we Pākehā must do with our own people. What if bodies like mine learned to 'let it breathe'—to cede control over what action is called for, to use the spaces and voices we have to give space for what we are not, and to move very slowly and carefully when it comes to those moments when we use the public platforms available to us? This feels especially important to learn in relation to a decolonial future in Aotearoa,

---

[20] Matike Mai Aotearoa, "He Whakaaro Here Whakaumu Mō Aotearoa/The Report of Matike Mai Aotearoa— The Independent Working Group on Constitutional Transformation." (Matike Mai Aotearoa, 2016), https://nwo.org.nz/wp-content/uploads/2018/06/MatikeMaiAotearoa25Jan16.pdf.

[21] Alexis Shotwell, "Bearing: Claiming Bad Kin", 2019, https://www.blackwoodgallery.ca//publications/sduk/bearing/claiming-bad-kin.

which, as Ani Mikaere as well as the Matike Mai Aotearoa report also emphasise, wherein tikanga Māori (protocols) offer a path to restoring everyone's honour and a means for non-Māori to belong, but only by Pākehā ceding control and becoming decentred.[22] Taking a step towards the challenges Hura offered did not require non-Māori substantiating, even speculatively, what deliberative designs might respond to those challenges. Rather, taking a step towards these challenges most fundamentally required conceding to being led, being guided by Māori regarding those aspirations and designs going forward. In this body so accustomed and incentivized to acting by filling space and engaging as expert, to truly listen here perhaps required, most of all, to acknowledge the differences in our positionalities in relation to the heartbreak, and the enormity of what it is we, by virtue of that position, do not understand or have the authority to say.

Bodies like mine can 'let it breathe' in a second sense, by moving away from conventional markers of and timelines for 'outcome' and 'impact' that can predominate in both non-Indigenous academics and activism. While of course tangible impacts are needed to transform an unjust world, particularly when presumed and sought within shorter time frames this expectation is one that is based in experiences of breathing easily. Drawing on interviews with Australian Aboriginal activists like Yorta Yorta woman Monica Morgan and Yorta Yorta man Bryan Andy, Clare Land makes a similar point regarding the common mistake among non-Indigenous allies of seeking immediate change with a sense of urgency, and frustration when it does not occur. This impatience for short term results "exist[s] in tension with the situation of Indigenous people running campaigns while also engaged in a day-to-day struggle to survive," as well as what can feel like 'laborious and time-consuming' protocols to care for relationships and responsibilities, as well death and grieving.[23] This push for productivity is also deeply connected to what Mark Rifkin calls 'settler time': capitalist, transactional, and extractive relations to temporality that are so hegemonic they can be largely insensible.[24] How might bodies like mine release the firm grip of such expectations for what outcome and action look like, so that our zeal to act and contribute to change does not in fact add further burdens and undermine the crucial work of 'survival [a]s a radical action,' or 'care as warfare'?[25] How might our own actions orient to supporting the

[22] Ani Mikaere, "Are We All New Zealanders Now? A Māori Perspective to the Pākehā Quest for Indigeneity", *The Bruce Jesson Foundation* (blog), 31 October 2004, https://www.brucejesson.com/ani-mikaere-2004-are-we-all-new-zealanders-now-a-maori-response-to-the-pakeha-quest-for-indigeneity/. Matike Mai Aotearoa, "He Whakaaro Here Whakaumu Mō Aotearoa/The Report of Matike Mai Aotearoa—The Independent Working Group on Constitutional Transformation."
[23] Clare Land, *Decolonizing Solidarity: Dilemmas and Directions for Supporters of Indigenous Struggles* (Zed Books Ltd., 2015), 169–70.
[24] Mark Rifkin, *Beyond Settler Time: Temporal Sovereignty and Indigenous Self-Determination* (Durham; London: Duke University Press, 2017).
[25] Sarah Ahmed, "Selfcare as Warfare", feministkilljoys, 25 August 2014, https://feministkilljoys.com/2014/08/25/selfcare-as-warfare/.

capacity of others to breathe more easily within the here and now, as a crucial part of the structural transformation required to redress systemic inequities of breath? And how might orienting to the particular economies of breath within our specific relationships keep us attuned to that broader structural context that is always-already in the interpersonal moment, so that we are able to "engag[e] with the humanity" of others who live in very different relationship to the heartbreak? This focus on 'letting it breathe' in this sense is a call to the highly particular, the specific people and relationships between us. It is a call to remember, as Te Kawehau Hoskins writes, bringing Levinas into dialogue with te ao Māori conceptions of relationality, that "*who* others are is always in excess of *what* they are".[26]

Finally, this experience highlighted a third way that bodies like mine can learn to 'let it breathe.' Clare Land and Jen Margaret, among others, caution that non-Indigenous would-be allies often fail to stay involved and active in solidarity with Indigenous communities over the longer term.[27] This tendency feels deeply connected to the capacity of such allies to 'opt in' to these struggles—they are struggles bodies like mine must learn, and continue to remember, to feel keenly, against the grain of both the collective amnesia of settler society and our own daily sense experiences of breathing easily.[28] In response to this pattern, non-Indigenous people are advised to "Listen, take direction and stick around".[29] This recent experience brought to light that this advice is also important for those moments when we get it wrong: the importance of learning to stand to take the criticism, and—though perhaps more cautiously, more behind the scenes, more humbly, and over time—to come back to keep working. Because absconding is easy, but also because learning is inevitably life-long, indeed intergenerational, and for a body like mine is more likely to entail trial and error, perhaps more is said of our character by what we do when challenged and corrected than by how correct our actions may be at the outset. How can we stay focused on the work of transforming an unjust world in these moments when Indigenous people are generous enough to take time to challenge and educate us to do better? Rather than fetishize a need to feel faultless which mobilises counter-productive 'settler moves to innocence',[30] how can we valorise the capacity to stand to hear these

---

[26] Te Kawehau Hoskins, "A Fine Risk: Ethics in Kaupapa Māori Politics", *New Zealand Journal of Educational Studies* 47, no. 2 (2012): 92.

[27] Jen Margaret, *Working as Allies: Supporters of Indigenous Justice Reflect* (Auckland: AWEA, 2013). Land, *Decolonizing Solidarity*, 166.

[28] Emily Beausoleil, "Listening to Claims of Structural Injustice", *Angelaki* 24, no. 4 (4 July 2019): 120–35. Emily Beausoleil, "'Gather Your People': Learning to Listen Intergenerationally in Settler-Indigenous Politics", *Political Theory* 48, no. 6 (1 December 2020): 665–91.

[29] Zainab Amadahy and Bonita Lawrence, "Indigenous Peoples and Black People in Canada: Settlers or Allies?", in *Breaching the Colonial Contract: Anti-Colonialism in the US and Canada*, ed. Arlo Kempf, Explorations of Educational Purpose (Dordrecht: Springer Netherlands, 2009), 105–36, https://doi.org/10.1007/978-1-4020-9944-1_7.

[30] Eve Tuck and K. Wayne Yang, "Decolonization Is Not a Metaphor", *Decolonization: Indigeneity, Education & Society* 1, no. 1 (8 September 2012), https://jps.library.utoronto.ca/index.php/des/article/view/18630.

challenges and remain in the sustained work of growing to meet them over a lifetime, indeed across generations? Rather than focus on the immediate moment, how can we take the long view as inheritors of an unjust world that lives and is sustained through the (un)sensed experiences of the body, as ancestors who have an opportunity to come to see and act to change how that inheritance shapes the future?

By virtue of being in this body, there is a great deal I still do not see. And I run the risk, in how I continue to read and respond to a world that unjustly lets me breathe easily within it, of causing further harm within gestures of solidarity. But as minor a movement, my hope is that learning to sense the vast distance between my own position and that of the heartbreak, and sense the deep-seated obliviousness to such distance, can mitigate such harm.

References

Ahmed, Sara. "Selfcare as Warfare". feministkilljoys, 25 August 2014. https://feministkilljoys.com/2014/08/25/selfcare-as-warfare/.

——— *Strange Encounters: Embodied Others in Post-Coloniality*. London: Routledge, 2000. https://doi.org/10.4324/9780203349700.

Amadahy, Zainab, and Bonita Lawrence. "Indigenous Peoples and Black People in Canada: Settlers or Allies?" In *Breaching the Colonial Contract: Anti-Colonialism in the US and Canada*, edited by Arlo Kempf, 105–36. Explorations of Educational Purpose. Dordrecht: Springer Netherlands, 2009. https://doi.org/10.1007/978-1-4020-9944-1_7.

Barnes, Helen Moewaka, Belinda Borell, and Time McCreanor. "Theorising the Structural Dynamics of Ethnic Privilege in Aotearoa: Unpacking 'This Breeze at My Back' (Kimmell and Ferber 2003)". *International Journal of Critical Indigenous Studies* 7, no. 1 (1 January 2014): 1–14. https://doi.org/10.5204/ijcis.v7i1.120.

Beausoleil, Emily. "'Gather Your People': Learning to Listen Intergenerationally in Settler-Indigenous Politics". *Political Theory* 48, no. 6 (1 December 2020): 665–91. https://doi.org/10.1177/0090591720919392.

——— "Listening to Claims of Structural Injustice". *Angelaki* 24, no. 4 (4 July 2019): 120–35. https://doi.org/10.1080/0969725X.2019.1635832.

Butler, Judith. *Frames of War: When Is Life Grievable?* London: Verso, 2009.

Cahill, Caitlin, and Rachel Pain. "Representing Slow Violence and Resistance: On Hiding and Seeing". *ACME: An International Journal for Critical Geographies* 18, no. 5 (3 October 2019): 1054–65.

Case, Emalani. *Everything Ancient Was Once New: Indigenous Persistence from Hawai'i to Kahiki*. Everything Ancient Was Once New. University of Hawaii Press, 2021. https://doi.org/10.1515/9780824888183.

Hoskins, Te Kawehau. "A Fine Risk: Ethics in Kaupapa Māori Politics", *New Zealand Journal of Educational Studies* 47, no. 2 (2012): 85–99.

Hura, Nadine Anne. "Please Bear with Me as 5,000 Words Is More My Comfort Zone so Twitter Is a Challenge but I Really Wanted to Add Some Whakaaro to This Discussion about the Spinoff Piece Written" by @MaxRashbrooke and @BeausoleilEmily on CAs.' Tweet. *Twitter,* 27 February 2020. https://twitter.com/nadineannehura/status/1233141388071489538.

——— "Totally! Oh… Not at All I Was Actually Just Reacting to the Whole Wide Kōrero and My Disappointment That the Authors Never Engaged with the Humanity of My Father and My Bro, Which Your Thread Highlighted for Me, but i'm New to Twitter so Sometimes Retweet the Wrong Thing Lol". Tweet. *Twitter,* 27 February 2020. https://twitter.com/nadineannehura/status/1233135200256684032.

——— "Who Gets to Be an 'Ordinary New Zealander'? On Citizens' Assemblies, Climate Change and Tangata Whenua". The Spinoff, 23 November 2019. https://thespinoff.co.nz/atea/23-11-2019/who-gets-to-be-an-ordinary-new-zealander-on-citizens-assemblies-climate-change-and-tangata-whenua.

Kimmel, Michael S. "Toward a Sociology of the Superordinate: This Breeze at My Back". In *Privilege: A Reader*, 4th Edition., 1–13. New York: Routledge, 2018.

Land, Clare. *Decolonizing Solidarity: Dilemmas and Directions for Supporters of Indigenous Struggles*. Zed Books Ltd., 2015.

Margaret, Jen. *Working as Allies: Supporters of Indigenous Justice Reflect*. Auckland: AWEA, 2013.

Matike Mai Aotearoa. "He Whakaaro Here Whakaumu Mō Aotearoa/The Report of Matike Mai Aotearoa—The Independent Working Group on Constitutional Transformation." Matike Mai Aotearoa, 2016. https://nwo.org.nz/wp-content/uploads/2018/06/MatikeMaiAotearoa25Jan16.pdf.

Medina, José. *The Epistemology of Resistance: Gender and Racial Oppression, Epistemic Injustice, and Resistant Imaginations*. 1st edition. Oxford: Oxford University Press, 2012.

Mikaere, Ani. "Are We All New Zealanders Now? A Māori Perspective to the Pākehā Quest for Indigeneity". *The Bruce Jesson Foundation* (blog), 31 October 2004. https://www.brucejesson.com/ani-mikaere-2004-are-we-all-new-zealanders-now-a-maori-response-to-the-pakeha-quest-for-indigeneity/.

Ngata, Tina. "All the Quals in the World Don't Matter". Tweet. *Twitter*, 28 February 2020. https://twitter.com/tinangata/status/1232870126711558145.

——— "Wow. @TheSpinoffTV Branching into Full-Blown Whitesplaining Now". Tweet. *Twitter*, 27 February 2020. https://twitter.com/tinangata/status/1232870126711558145.

Nixon, Rob. *Slow Violence and the Environmentalism of the Poor*. Cambridge, Mass: Harvard University Press, 2011.

Rifkin, Mark. *Beyond Settler Time: Temporal Sovereignty and Indigenous Self-Determination*. Durham; London: Duke University Press, 2017.

——— *Settler Common Sense: Queerness and Everyday Colonialism in the American Renaissance*. 1st edition. Minneapolis; London: University of Minnesota Press, 2014.

Sherwood-O'Regan, Kera. "Yeah Super Cringey... like Umm on What Authority Are You Speaking on Matike Mai & Why Do a Response All This Time Later When You Haven't Actually Been Engaging with Our Communities on What Kōrero Have Been Happening since Nadine's Piece AND When You Have No Skin in the Game?" Tweet. *Twitter*, 27 February 2020. https://twitter.com/keraoregan/status/1232888520999493632.

Shotwell, Alexis. "Bearing: Claiming Bad Kin", 2019. https://www.blackwoodgallery.ca//publications/sduk/bearing/claiming-bad-kin.

Sleeter, Christine. "Inheriting Footholds and Cushions: Family Legacies and Institutional Racism". *Counterpoints* 449 (2014): 11–26.

Tuck, Eve, and K. Wayne Yang. "Decolonization Is Not a Metaphor". *Decolonization: Indigeneity, Education & Society* 1, no. 1 (8 September 2012). https://jps.library.utoronto.ca/index.php/des/article/view/18630.

Contributors

Basel Abbas and Ruanne Abou-Rahme
work together across a range of sound, image, text, installation and performance practices. Their practice is engaged with the intersections between performativity, political imaginaries, the body and virtuality. Across their works, they probe a contemporary landscape marked by seemingly perpetual crisis and an endless 'present', one that is shaped by a politics of desire and disaster. They have been developing a body of work that questions this suspension of the present and searches for ways in which an altogether different imaginary and language can emerge that is not bound within a colonial/capitalist narrative and discourse. In their projects they find themselves excavating, activating and inventing incidental narratives, figures, gestures and sites as material for re-imagining the possibilities of the present. They are often reflecting on ideas of non-linearity in the form of returns, amnesia and déjà vu, and in the process unfolding the slippages between actuality and projection (fiction, myth, wish), what is and what could be. Their approach has largely been one of sampling materials both existing and self-authored in the form of sound, image, text, objects and recasting them into altogether new 'scripts'. The result is a practice that investigates the political, visceral, material possibilities of sound, image, text and site, taking the form of multi-media installations and live sound/image performances. https://www.baselandruanne.com/

Emily Beausoleil
is a Senior Lecturer of Politics at Te Herenga Waka-Victoria University of Wellington, Editor-in-Chief of *Democratic Theory* journal, and 2021 recipient of Royal Society Te Āparangi's Early Career Researcher Award for Social Sciences. As a political theorist, she explores the conditions, challenges, and creative possibilities for democratic engagement in diverse societies, with particular attention to the capacity for 'voice' and listening in conditions of inequality. Current community collaborations

include co-design and lead coordination of the nationwide anti-racism programme Tauiwi Tautoko, independent evaluation of the creation of a Te Tiriti-led climate assembly, and artistic collaboration with theatre and film makers to incite receptivity and response to the lived struggles navigating New Zealand's Work and Income system. Her work has been published in *Political Theory, Contemporary Political Theory, Constellations, Conflict Resolution Quarterly,* and *Ethics & Global Politics*, as well as various books. Her first book, *Staging Democracy: When and How Performance Becomes Democratic Politics* (De Gruyter) will launch a new book series (Critical Thinking and Contemporary Politics) in 2023.

Hope Ginsburg
in her long-term, interdisciplinary projects prioritizes experiential learning and collaboration. She has exhibited nationally and internationally at venues such as MoMA PS1, MASS MoCA, Wexner Center for the Arts, USF Contemporary Art Museum, Baltimore Museum of Art, KW Institute for Contemporary Art, and Contemporary Art Center Vilnius. Her projects have received support from the National Endowment for the Arts, The Andy Warhol Foundation for the Visual Arts, and Women & Philanthropy at The Ohio State University. She is the recipient of a Wexner Center for the Arts Artist Residency Award, Virginia Museum of Fine Arts Fellowship, and Art Matters Foundation Grant. Ginsburg has attended residencies such as the Robert Rauschenberg Residency, Skowhegan, the Wexner Center Film/Video Studio Program, and The Harbor at Beta-Local. She is a professor at Virginia Commonwealth University School of the Arts and lives and works on Tsenacomoco land (Richmond, Virginia, USA). https://www.hopeginsburg.com/

Miriam Jakob
is a choreographer, performer and artist/researcher based in Berlin. She playfully addresses questions of representation, accessibility and inter-species communication through installations, film and collaborative stage works. Her choreographic language interweaves autobiographical anecdotes and affective experiences with socio-political as well as ecological topics. As part of the Berlin Artistic Research Grant Programme/gkfd of the Berlin Senate she co-developed a participatory artistic format of breath work called *Breathing With* together with her colleague Jana Unmüßig. She graduated from the MA DAS Choreography at the Academy of Theatre and Dance Amsterdam, the BA in Dance, Context, Choreography at HZT Inter-University Centre for Dance Berlin and holds an MA in Anthropology from the FU Berlin. https://miriamjakob.com/

Shahram Khosravi
is a former taxi driver and is currently an accidental Professor of Anthropology at Stockholm University. He is the author of several books, such as: *After Deportation: Ethnographic Perspectives* (Palgrave, 2017, edited volume); *Young and Defiant in Tehran* (University of Pennsylvania Press, 2008); *The Illegal Traveler: an auto-ethnography of borders* (Palgrave, 2010); *Precarious Lives: Waiting and Hope in Iran* (University of Pennsylvania Press, 2017); *Waiting. A project in Conversation* (transcript, 2021, edited volume), and *Seeing Like a Smuggler* (Pluto Press, 2022, edited volume). Khosravi has been an active writer in the international press. He is a co-founder of *Critical Border Studies*, a network for scholars and artists.

Bojana Kunst
is a philosopher, dramaturge and performance theoretician. She works as a professor at the Institute for Applied Theatre Studies in Justus Liebig University Giessen, where she heads the international master's program, Choreography and Performance. She was as a researcher at the University of Ljubljana and the University of Antwerp (till 2009), and later a guest professor at the University of Hamburg (2009–2012). She has lectured and organized seminars, workshops and laboratories in different academic institutions, theatres and artistic organisations across Europe, and has worked continuously with independent artistic initiatives, artists, groups and activists. Her research interests are contemporary performance and dance, arts theory and philosophy of contemporary art. She published *Artist at Work, Proximity of Art and Capitalism* (Zero Books, 2015), and *The Life of Art. Transversal Lines of Care* (in Slovenian, Maska, 2021).

Francesca Raimondi
lives in Berlin and Amsterdam and is assistant Professor of Philosophy at the Art Academy in Düsseldorf. Her interdisciplinary research and teaching are located at the intersection of political theory, critical social theory, feminism and aesthetics, with a special focus on modern forms of embodiment, their critique and transformation through artistic practices. Among her latest publications are the edited volume (with Martina Dobbe) *Serialität und Wiederholung: Revisited* (Matthes & Seitz, 2021) on seriality and repetition in contemporary art, and the essay *The spectral present of control and the strategies of performance* (in: *Aesthetic Temporalities Today,* eds. Gabriele Genge et.al., transcript, 2020).

Jana Unmüßig
moves within a post-disciplinary understanding of making and considers various practices central to the construction of her artistic identity (e.g. the practice of painting, the practice of parenting, the practice of reading, the practice of wondering, the practice of teaching.) She works as part-time lecturer on the MA Choreography at Uniarts Helsinki and acts as visiting researcher at the Performing Arts Research Center of the same institution. https://jana-unmussig.com/

The team of the publication series *Corporeal Matters*

Daniel Belasco Rogers
was born in London in 1966. He has worked as a designer, director, composer and performer for experimental theatre and performance since 1989. After moving to Berlin, he established the artist duo *plan b* in 2002, together with Sophia New. As well as making durational performances, installations, social interventions and new media projects, Sophia and Daniel have a practice of recording every journey they make with a GPS. Daniel was a member of the Junge Akademie at the Akademie der Künste in 2006 and has taken part in artist residencies in Germany, Austria, the UK and Norway. Daniel has held practical artistic workshops in Tokyo, Sao Paulo, Banff (Canada), Beijing and many other European cities and taught as a guest lecturer in higher educational institutions across Europe. As a performer and collaborator, he has worked with She She Pop, Club Real, Gob Squad, Forced Entertainment, Sabine Zahn and Juan Domínguez/Arantxa Martínez. He is currently a guest professor at the Universität der Künste Berlin. https://planbperformance.net

Janez Janša
is a professor at HZT Berlin and a contemporary artist who focuses on the relationship between art and the social and political context in his performance, conceptual and interdisciplinary art works. His particular areas of research are the performativity of name, the relationship between art and war, as well as time and temporalities in art and life. He was the director of *Maska* (1998–2021), an institute for publishing, artistic production and education based in Ljubljana, Slovenia, and founder and editor of two book series and several readers on contemporary dance and theatre. He was editor-in-chief of *Maska Performing Arts Journal* (1999–2006). He is the author of a book on Jan Fabre's early work: (*La discipline du chaos, le chaos de la discipline*, 1994). Janez

is a co-founder and the first president of the association of freelance artists *Asociacija* in Slovenia and a member of the editorial boards of the journals *Performance Research* and *Maska*. In 2007, together with two other Slovenian artists, he changed his previous name into the name of the conservative three-time prime minister of Slovenia. Together with Janez Janša and Janez Janša, he is the owner of the Janez Janša® registered trade mark.

Ana Lessing Menjibar

is a German-Spanish performer, choreographer, multidisciplinary artist and art director, born and based in Berlin. In her interdisciplinary practice, she interweaves body, sound worlds and language in multimedia installations in which she experiments with the transformative potential of flamenco in the context of contemporary dance and performance. She graduated from the performance art Master's program, Solo/Dance/Authorship at HZT Berlin. Previously she studied Visual Communication at the University of the Arts Berlin and has worked as an art director and publisher in the field of culture and art for many years. Amongst many other places, Ana Lessing Menjibar has performed, directed or exhibited at Uferstudios Berlin, Sophiensaele, Komische Oper Berlin, tanzhaus nrw, and the Kammermusiksaal der Berliner Philharmonie, at Villa Romana (Italy), PHotoEspaña or at the Centre Pompidou Málaga (Spain). https://analessingmenjibar.com

Sandra Noeth

is a professor at HZT Berlin and internationally active as a curator and dramaturge. She specializes in ethical and political perspectives of body practice and theory and in dramaturgy in dance and performance. Many of her research projects are transdisciplinary in nature, including *Violence of Inscriptions*, a program series on bodies under structural violence with A. Zaides in 2016–18 at HAU Hebbel am Ufer; *What does it take to cross a border?* in 2019 at Ifa Gallery Berlin; *Bodies, un-protected* on the relation between bodies, art and protection in 2020–22 with Künstlerhaus Mousonturm; *Hållning*—a practice-led proposal for collective learning and action in 2021 with MDT, the Goethe Institute Stockholm, ABF Stockholm University of the Arts. Sandra acted as Head of Dramaturgy and Research at the Tanzquartier Wien between 2009–2014, where she co-edited the periodical *SCORES* from 2010–16. Further publications include *Embodiment: Violence* (ed. with PARSE journal, 2022, online); *Bodies of Evidence: Ethics, Aesthetics, and Politics of Movement* (2018, with G. Ertem, Passagen); *Resilient Bodies, Residual Effects: Artistic Articulations of*

Borders and Collectivity from Lebanon and Palestine (2019, transcript); *The Performance of Worldmaking in Dance and Choreography* (ed. with G. Klein, 2011, transcript).

Sandra Umathum
is a theatre and performance scholar as well as a dramaturge. From 2019 to 2022, she was a Professor for (Applied) Theory Dance, Choreography, Performance at HZT Berlin. Before that, she held a professorship for Theatre Studies and Dramaturgy at the Ernst Busch Academy of Dramatic Arts in Berlin (2013–2018) and a guest professorship for Dramaturgy at the University of Music and Theatre Felix Mendelssohn Bartholdy in Leipzig (2010–2012). She is the author of *Kunst als Aufführungserfahrung*, a book on intersubjective experiences in the visual arts (transcript, 2011), and has co-edited, among other publications, *Disabled Theater* (diaphanes, 2015) and *Postdramaturgien* (Neofelis, 2020). Her research focuses on the theory and practice of contemporary theatre and performance on illness, disability and non-normative bodies in performance, on performance and/as documentation, on shooting (with guns and with cameras), and on new forms of dramaturgy.

Imprint

Corporeal Matters

Series Editors
Janez Janša, Sandra Noeth & Sandra Umathum

Book no. 1
BREATHE
Critical Research into the Inequalities of Life

Editors
Sandra Noeth & Janez Janša

Authors
Basel Abbas & Ruanne Abou-Rahme
Emily Beausoleil
Hope Ginsburg
Miriam Jakob & Jana Unmüßig
Shahram Khosravi
Bojana Kunst
Francesca Raimondi

Design Ana Lessing Menjibar
Design Support Peter Löffelholz
Copy Editing Daniel Belasco Rogers
Printed by Majuskel Medienproduktion GmbH, Wetzlar
Print-ISBN 978-3-8376-6650-2
PDF-ISBN 978-3-8394-6650-6

Breathe: Critical Research into the Inequalities of Life is based on the MA SODA lecture series curated by Sandra Noeth at HZT Berlin in the study year 2020–21.
The publication is financially supported by the UdK—Berlin University of the Arts and the HZT—Inter-University Centre for Dance Berlin.

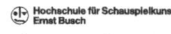